AF265104

"In "The Art of Persuasive Influence" Glen Sharkey will take you on a fascinating journey into human relationships where kindness, care, respect, and empathy triumph over negativity. A powerful and refreshing take on the subject of Influence."
Nabil Doss, Expert in Influential Communication, 2016-2017 President of the Global Speakers Federation

"Glen is perfectly placed to write this important book on influence largely because he is someone that has lived it out. He is a leader whose care for those he is leads is genuine, empowering and persuasive."
Michael McQueen, Five-time bestselling author, Nevin Award Winner

"I love this book full of real life experiences, personal lessons and insights from years in the training room and on the job. Sharkey has captured in a short easy read what some authors take books and more books to cover. The Art of Persuasive Influence is leadership distilled down to easy to grasp key principles that will serve you whether you're an emerging or experienced leader in any field - a salient reminder of what really matters for us all"
Simon Wickham, Ex CEO of Yachting NZ, CEO of The Trusts

Glen is skilled at being able to take everyday encounters and turn them into a compelling read. Clear, succinct, and born from a lifetime of experience he is proficient at giving endless examples of the art of persuasive influence. He writes not only to the intellectual mind but heart also. A useful, helpful book to help us all live life well. Many books promise to change your life. This one will also enable you to influence other people's lives as well.

Allison Mooney, Award-Winning Speaker/Author

"Glen Sharkey walks the talk. He uses simple, everyday encounters and examples to get his points across. He does this brilliantly in person and I would encourage you to make the time, the investment and effort to see Glen in action as a speaker. What is really astounding is Sharkey's ability to connect with us through the written word. His stories, encounters and examples very quickly leap off the page and unlock our memories. We get the chance to relive everyday events once more. But this time we are reliving them with the consideration of Sharkey's advice. He makes us reconsider our decision-making process and factor in simple truths. He makes us want to make better decisions. Big ones and small ones. Glen Sharkey does indeed walk the talk, he influences us. Better than anyone else I know."

David Nottage, World Toastmasters Champion, Winner 2009, 2010, 2011 People's Choice Awards 'Best National Training Provider', Director of Torque Business

"Glen walks his talk and this book is a great example of his practical, no nonsense and fun approach to coaching, training and life. This is an essential read if you are in any position to work with or indeed live with other people to whom you influence."

Karen Tui Boyes, NZ Business Woman of the Year, CEO Spectrum Education

"This book is loaded with down to earth examples and easy to implement ideas to help increase your influence. Using every day situations, Glen provides concrete evidence on the kind of behaviours and traits you need to become a better leader and a better part of a team. So many valuable lessons that it will be your new 'go to resource' that you can use time and time again."

Warwick Merry, President Professional Speakers Australia, CEO of Get More Pty Ltd

"In a particularly open and honest fashion Sharkey shares stories from his own life to illustrate influencing skills that can work for everyone. One by one these real life moments fashion an authentic read and one that is particularly relevant in an age of criticism and negativity. In "The Art of Persuasive Influence" Sharkey provides the reader with tools to turn things round in the best possible manner. From the workplace to the home there is nothing too high or unattainable in what he suggests. These are stories for you and for me in a time where good influence is needed most ".

Andrew Hoggard, Country Manager Dentsply

"From the current President of NSANZ and the Educator of the Year (2015/6), who has worked with thousands of people over three decades, comes a practical and insightful guide on influencing people for positive outcomes. It's filled with examples from his own life and from those that he has trained and it is sure to help you lift your own persuasive game!"

Mike Handcock, Chairman of Rock Your Life, Founder of The Conscious Leadership Movement

"Glen Sharkey's latest book, 'The Art of Persuasive Influence', offers a wealth of knowledge gleaned from actual everyday experience, not from a textbook, and therefore it offers invaluable advice to deal with all types of leadership challenges. The book is written to be accessible to everyone, whatever their leader role may be – in the workplace, the sportsground, at home – and contains a huge number of ideas and suggestions to allow the reader to become a positive influence on those around them. I would strongly urge anyone who is a leader to read, learn and grow in their role. A great read."
John Shackleton, Masters Swimming Champion and Award Winning Speaker

"Glen Sharkey is an expert when it comes to leadership and his life experiences and stories shine bright in this book, providing substance and validation to the subject of relationship influence. Using 30 years of experience in developing people Glen Sharkey has created a book full of real life examples that will help you develop meaningful relationships through care and courage, gaining you long term respect, trust and influence amongst your peers and community. There are no shortcuts to doing life well and that message is delivered clearly here. 'The Art of Persuasive Influence' is a must read for individuals, partners, parents, leaders and employers alike."
Andrew Chambers, Director of Eightfold Financial Services

"Glen is able to bring his book alive by sharing a lot of personal stories and experiences from his training sessions. This make the book really easy to read and very practical. You can immediately translate more

general concepts like 'caring' or 'courage' into day to day situations and apply them in your own life. If you want to have an influence on others in a genuine and positive way, this book is a must-read."
Cyriel Kortleven, CSP Belgium, International Speaker

"In his new book "The Art of Persuasive Influence" Glen Sharkey has given us a practical, real life, training solution. The insights given in this book will make your team rethink their ideas on leadership. This book is a mini encyclopaedia of 'how to' ideas. Insightful and eye opening!"
Bill James, NZ Business Speaker of the Year 2012, NSANZ Speaker of the Year 2015-2016

"As a relationship management specialist I love this book. Glen Sharkey is not only a brilliant keynote speaker, he is a brilliant author too. In this book he has captured the essence of influence. As Glen says in his book; "The giving and taking of influence is the basis of relationships". I could not agree more! Not only that - he goes on to detail how to use influence, when to use it and how to do it ethically. It's an easy read, yet packed with useful, practical and ready to implement models, strategies and ideas. Great work Glen!"
Lindsay Adams CSP, Global Speaking Fellow, CEO Teamocracy, 2009-2010 President, Global Speakers Federation Life Member, Nevin Award Winner, Past National President, Professional Speakers Australia

"Glen Sharkey has a knack of reflecting his being in the written word.

This book is a guiding light for all of us who seek to influence, written in an easy Sunday afternoon walk style. Glen's storytelling is artful and poignant."
Chris Taylor, Director of "Winning Habits"

"Glen's book is a practical, no fuss perspective on persuasion. Using real world examples, Glen shows the way to effectively influence with integrity."
Jon Yeo, TEDx Melbourne Curator

"The Art of Persuasive Influence by Glen Sharkey is an excellent resource to help you positively influence the people and outcomes you regularly come across in both your business and personal life. From assessing 'pain points' through to his innovative 'care model', Glen's exciting book helps you to put in place authentic strategies to develop levels of influence that can positively shape lives. Filled with amusing anecdotes and real life stories that add real value to the reader, this book, I am sure, will become an instant classic."
Tom O'Neil, New Zealand Herald Columnist, Best-selling international author and multi-award-winning speaker

ALSO BY GLEN SHARKEY

Discover the Keys to Training Excellence

30+ Activities to Take Your Training to the Next Level

Fairly Common Tales: Fables for Leaders in the Workplace

The Art of Persuasive
INFLUENCE

The Lifeworks Co Ltd

The Art of Persuasive
INFLUENCE

*What works and why
in positively influencing
people and outcomes*

Glen Sharkey

The Lifeworks Co Ltd

TABLE OF CONTENTS

DEDICATION

I want to thank my wife Jenny for teaching me that being open to the influence of others is a powerful way to build connection in strong relationships. I am so indebted to you!

PREFACE

When I first began drafting this book I had every intention of it being specifically about leadership. I wanted to encourage and inspire leaders in the workplace through my own experiences in terms of leading people and teams, my experience of being led by leaders including the good the bad and the not-so-pretty, the experience of other leaders both personally known to me and somewhat more famous, and anecdotes from my leadership training programs over the years. But the more I wrote the more I realised that the stories that I began to record clearly had an application to a much wider audience than simply those who have a formal leadership position in the workplace.

I've spent my adult life training people. One of the organisations that I deliver leadership training to has a nationally known ex-All Black rugby captain as their company's ambassador. As part of the training program I show a video on safety and leadership in the organisation. This nationally known rugby celebrity commentates the video and early on he makes the statement *"Leadership is about influence - nothing more, nothing less."* This mirrors what I have been saying for several years to those people who attend my leadership programs who are not currently in formal positions of leadership. It is important that I frame their training experience as honing their ability to influence those around them. In this way, I can prepare them for the leadership roles the company sees that they have the potential to fulfil in the future.

Influence may be a synonym for leadership, but it is not merely confined to formal leadership roles in the workplace. As this book will articulate, influence occurs in families, with customers, with neighbours, on the sports field with fellow players and the opposition and even the referee or umpire. In fact, influence is seen at its clearest when it occurs for the ***benefit of both parties*** without any positional authority in the relationship.

The Art of Persuasive
INFLUENCE

CHAPTER ONE

ATTITUDE

INTRODUCTION

I love delivering leadership training. It's been my career now, in some form or other, for the past thirty years of my life. I have delivered leadership training to children, teenagers, adults and the elderly, across diverse ethnicities. I've given training to people who never even completed their schooling, and those with PhD's. I've presented to the poorest of the poor and to CEO's of multi-million dollar corporations. After all these experiences one thing has become patently clear to me: **leadership is influence**.

Influence is defined as 'having an effect upon' people, objects, or circumstances. When we influence another person, we have an effect upon them – on their behaviour, thinking, and emotions. As a result of this effect, a ripple on effect often occurs where the situations and circumstances surrounding these people are also influenced. Influence is powerful. It has the power for tremendous positive impact in an ongoing manner across multiple domains.

The Merriam-Webster Dictionary defines influence as: "The act or power of producing an effect without apparent exertion of force or direct exercise of command". This definition reflects the aim of this book to help you reduce your effort when it comes to influencing others, so that influence is accomplished without apparent exertion, and to create a change in others without commanding it or forcing it. This book is about the ***power of influence to create self-responsibility in others.***

Of course, it is possible to influence people to their detriment, which might more accurately be termed 'manipulation'. Manipulation is using influence to get people to do what is beneficial for yourself. Influence, in my definition, is motivating people to do what is beneficial for themselves and those around them. Manipulation is disempowering. Influence is empowering. This book expresses continually that these tools be used to influence people both for your betterment and theirs.

Some of the work that I do involves facilitating programs with operational staff who are not in any form of official leadership. When I deliver leadership programs to 'pre-leaders' I emphasise that before we can lead others we need to learn to lead ourselves. Leading and influencing others, and even accepting the influence of others, are behaviours determined in part by an individual's ability to influence themselves. This book will share valuable insights as to what constitutes influence and how we can more effectively learn to hone our abilities in this area for our own benefit, and for the benefit of those we are attempting to influence.

CHOOSE YOUR MOOD

To be effective and maximize your leadership influence on those around you it is necessary that you choose your attitude. As a leader, you are not only required to model great attitude, but also to model and coach others in the process of choosing their attitudes. *Fostering a culture where people take responsibility for their own attitudes is a key to effective leadership*.

Own Your Attitude

I was taking a leadership program some time ago and I had a subject matter expert come and speak to my group on sales and marketing. This person was a key account manager for a business with thousands of employees. He dealt with very large customers and very large contracts. Because the business was part of a logistics company, it was not always possible to deliver to customers as per arrangement because of human shortcoming and external factors such as adverse environmental conditions. The manager would therefore find himself from time to time in the frustrating and embarrassing position of having to face customers with the news that his company had failed to deliver. Being aware of this I asked the manager how he managed those situations where he was essentially the meat in the sandwich between the client and his operators, knowing that the failure to deliver almost never his fault directly. I'll never forget his response, which I immediately wrote onto the flipchart that I was using in the classroom. His reply was *"I choose my mood."* It was such a simple but profound response.

The manager was aware in those situations that he had very little to bargain with, other than apologies and plausible reasons, however, he was also aware that he could choose the way that he felt, and that this choice would influence the overall result. He was much more likely to constructively influence the situation by shifting his mood from being embarrassed, frustrated, and even potentially ashamed, to being as positive as he could and adopting a 'can do' attitude. He knew that the embarrassment, frustration or guilt that he felt as a result of his company failing to deliver to the client would not do anything to change the circumstances. In fact, those feelings might motivate him to deflect the problem or deny responsibility for it. Instead, the manager chose an attitude of positivity and a focus on problem solving.

When someone comes to me with frustration about their team's inability to deliver, it feels to me like they are actually adding to the problem rather than trying to deliver me a solution, and in that case, I can't help but trust the person a little bit less. *People don't like to be influenced by those who are unwilling to take ownership*. In fact, not only do I prefer to deal with someone who is willing to take ownership for providing a solution rather than excuses, but when I see someone who has chosen a positive mood in the light of very challenging circumstances, that's precisely the type of person that I want to work with, and will be willing to be influenced by.

A Positive Attitude Changes Everything

Attitude is the 'be all and end all' in terms of influencing ourselves and those around us. A positive attitude is one of the most influential attitudes of all. I am personally much more open to the influence of positive, 'glass half full' people than I am to those who have a negative attitude and are gifted at seeing problems rather than solutions. When someone is trying to influence me, particularly when they are trying to shift my thinking or my behaviour, it can be hard enough for me to accept their influence without the additional burden of having to also wade through their negativity. ***Positivity opens both my ears and my heart to other people's thinking and perspective,*** whereas negative attitudes are much more likely to result in resistance and defensiveness.

I regularly train people who are frustrated in some way with their manager or up line leader. We all know how demoralizing it can be working under negative, dishonest or self-centred managers. But one thing I say to people who bring up their frustration is that as leaders ourselves we must take ultimate responsibility for our own attitude first, regardless of the external pressures to act otherwise. In the classroom, I will discuss the kinds of strategies that can be employed to manage our attitude, such as being solution focused, not sweating the small stuff, maintaining patience, seeing issues from other people's perspectives, and maintaining gratitude. Above all of these is the simplicity of realizing that your own attitude may have slipped, and making a straightforward decision to turn it around.

Alcoholics Anonymous uses an acronym; "HALT". HALT outlines the circumstances in which AA members are most likely to have their sobriety tested: when they are *Hungry, Angry, Lonely, and Tired*. Similarly, it's important that you and I know our 'touch points'-

those triggers which can and most likely will lead to a downward slide in our own attitude. It's much easier to turn a slipping attitude around when it's early into its slide, before it builds up momentum and we're trying to undo an avalanche.

Every person will at some point find themselves struggling with a negative attitude. We are all infallible humans. It gives us grace for ourselves when we recognise that sometimes our attitude is faltering simply because we are experiencing normal human stressors – such as hunger, frustration, isolation or tiredness. Sometimes our attitude slip is not because we have a bad attitude but because we are human. If we address the stressors, we often find it a lot easier to address our attitudes. But stressors aside, *we are all capable of attitude change*. Like most things in life, sometimes we just need to practice in order to build up our capacity in this area.

I wonder if, like me, you've ever been feeling grumpy, stressed, or upset, while sitting in a public place - maybe in an airport lounge or in an event venue where you had your guard down? At the end of a long day I have been sitting in an airport lounge – finally finishing up my phone calls and emails - finally alone with my tired-out attitude - when someone suddenly calls out my name and I'm face to face with a major client. What do I do – I put my 'game face' on! I make sure my attitude lines up with what this person deserves from their interaction with me. We've all done it. The key point is that we are capable, in a split second, of altering our mood and our attitude. In fact, sometimes the change is 180 degrees from dark to light (and if the client could have had a good, long look at our face prior to calling out, they'd be able to attest to the tectonic shift). This is a classic example of our ability to quickly shift our attitude and change our mood when we have a good enough reason.

A few years ago, I was working with a new client delivering customer service training. My wife's uncle, who was a reasonably young and very high profile Supreme Court judge, had died overnight. This was a complete shock for the family. Within hours of his death, my wife's aunt, the judge's sister, also died. Another complete shock. Two unexpected close family deaths within 24 hours of each other. Obviously, it was harder on my wife, but I really felt it also as I'd enjoyed a friendship with both of them for over 25 years by that stage. It was a devastating blow to the family, and yet I had to carry on and facilitate the training I was contracted to be doing. It certainly wasn't easy delivering happy, bouncy customer service training to this group when I was feeling grief over the loss, but I was compelled to choose my mood so that I might maximize my impact and influence with the client.

I'm not unique in going to work and delivering a service shortly after losing a close family member - many people have done it under far more trying circumstances than mine. It just serves as another reminder that we *do* have the ability to choose our mood.

Being able to choose the mood that you are feeling, or at the very least believing that it is possible to shift our attitudinal state, has two applications to the concept of influence. The first is that if we believe we can, and are, able to choose our mood then we have influence over ourselves. ***People who can influence themselves have a much greater chance of influencing others*** because they are role modelling the ability to change. Secondly, through the practice of choosing their attitude, these people become more cognisant of the process of change than those who are resistant to shifting their own behaviour or attitude.

Go to Your Room!!

When I was young I worked for an organisation where I noticed what, I felt, were questionable decisions being made in terms of financial administration at a governance level. This bothered me to the extent that, along with another staff member, I questioned the senior management on their financial principles. My questioning became so troublesome to the management that finally they decided to dismiss every staff member and have them reapply for their jobs in an effort to fire me and the other protagonist (without actually legally firing us). It was certainly a dubious move for them to make from a legal standpoint, not to mention the distrust it generated among all the staff, yet it happened and every staff member found themselves being interviewed for exactly the same job they had just been made redundant from. Every single staff member that is except the two of us who had questioned their financial practice. As I was actually very good at my job, I was eventually made an offer of being reinstated into my position if I would cease my protests and questioning. In those days, I wasn't one to back down from a confrontation.

As I processed through what to do I found myself at home one evening discussing the situation with a good friend of mine. My friend was older than me - and unquestionably wiser. He advised that I should learn to pick my battles – to be more strategic about what was really important to me and what I could learn to live with given it wasn't my responsibility or position to run the business the way I felt it should be run. In fact, the words that he used were, ***"You don't have to die on every cross - on every hill"***, and because I trusted and respected him I decided to drop my questioning, accept the reinstatement of my position and tone down my protests. Despite this my attitude was still not what it needed to be.

At the time, I was responsible for a large team of people and because of the way in which I structured the team and my work, every six weeks or so I would have a week long break from organising my team members when they worked remotely. I would simply be responsible for catching up and planning for the next six-week period. I had enough autonomy in the position to be able to organise my work this way normally, but because management was still unhappy with my attitude and with my unwillingness to align myself with their decisions, I was told to use my week without my team around to spend some time cleaning up the organisation's resource room.

I didn't respond well to this request - deeming the task irrelevant to my job description. It was the kind of job that would normally be given to interns or people from school on work experience, and I understood it to be a test of my willingness to submit to authority. It started to chew me up inside. I felt my motivation drop and my mood darken.

Despite, or maybe because of this, I managed to have some kind of revelation that **my attitude is my responsibility** and mine alone. While I had originally intended to contest the request, I instead adjusted my plan to 'gritting my teeth and bearing it'. However, that did little to address the ensuing resentment I felt towards management.

Fortunately for me, the 'light went on' inside me and I suddenly thought to myself; "Why am *I* allowing my attitude to be effected so dramatically?" A menial task, regardless of the agenda of those making me do it, was actually insufficient reason to alter my mood so dramatically. Ironically, at that time I had a quote on my wall at work which said; "Chasing the snake that bit you will only push the poison faster through your system!" So, I opted instead to make a 180-degree change in my attitude, and rather than do the bare minimum, I would perform the best resource room clean up that I was capable of.

With my reformed attitude, I undertook a task which should have taken no more than half a day, and spent three solid days - not only tidying up a shambles but also formulating and implementing new and helpful processes such as a video cataloguing system. At the end of the three days I felt proud of the job I'd done and the attitude I had maintained. Management were shocked at the turn around in my attitude and I felt 'in control' once again.

As a side note, before my turn-around I had applied for another job – at the time hoping to escape the situation I was in. The new job wasn't necessarily a job that I wanted, I just knew where I didn't want to be and saw it as a 'get out of jail' card. I never heard back regarding my application but it didn't matter - things had significantly improved and tensions had all but disappeared in my current role after I had managed to turn my attitude around. As it so happened the vacancy that I had applied for closed up so an appointment was never actually made, but seven months later I was called up and asked if I was still interested in the position. By this stage I had actually developed an excellent working relationship with management where I was and there was no longer a need to leave to 'escape'. However, I decided to accept the new position with the new company but this time had the full support of my current management and left on very good terms. In hindsight, I'm glad I didn't get offered the position prior to having the enormous attitude adjustment which was an incredibly important life lesson for me.

Most of us are much more willing to deal with and be influenced by someone who is cheerful and positive than by someone who is critical and negative. ***People will always prefer to be influenced by someone who is willing to take ownership*** by providing a solution to the problem at hand. A problem requires little effort to expose and point out. Dealing positively with the problem requires a lot more effort. When we see someone who has chosen a positive mood in the light of very challenging circumstances, it inspires trust. That is precisely the type of person that I want to work with, and someone I am open to being influenced by. Positivity pre-disposes us to trust. Negativity on the other hand, makes people nervous to be around us, unsure if we might be the next target of our unhappiness.

ATTITUDE DETERMINES ALTITUDE

The attitude with which we approach people will define the degree of influence we have with them. In the previous story regarding my own 180-degree shift, if I hadn't made such a shift I would have had absolutely no ability to influence my management because my poor attitude would have meant that I had behaved in a way that would have completely shut them down to anything I'd have to say.

One of my favourite quotes is that of South African president Nelson Mandela who, after 27 years of being unjustly incarcerated said; ***"Resentment is like drinking a cup of poison and hoping it will kill your enemies."*** Mandela was well aware of the capacity for his own bitterness to ruin his life. He had, however, practised having a positive attitude so many times, that when it came to choosing his attitude towards the members of a racist regime that stole almost three decades of his life, he could choose forgiveness.

This capacity for choosing and maintaining a positive and constructive attitude meant that Mandela was able to exercise seismic influence on an entire nation. No one wants to listen to someone with a bad attitude. The irony is that when you think you're right and everyone else is wrong, no one wants to hear about your superior way of thinking anyway. Being right on its own may not give you influence with others, but being right while practising a positive attitude very often will. You may have the best idea since sliced bread, or have the answer to everyone's most important questions, but the human hearing system seems to have a way of filtering out the opinions of the conceited. It may seem counterintuitive to an egotistical person but the fact of the matter often is that if they were to downgrade their opinion a notch or two, they would increase their chances of being heard and thereby of influencing those around them.

My childhood was not easy. I didn't have positive role models to show me how to choose my attitude early on. I grew up with a lot of negativity and learned to be quite a practitioner myself. My adult life has been a long journey of becoming increasingly aware of my negative tendencies and developing and utilising strategies for overcoming them. By the time I had reached my early twenties I genuinely thought that people were impressed by my knowledge and that it didn't matter *how* I voiced my opinion. As long as I was convinced that my thinking was superior to the opinions of those around me, I thought I had all that was necessary to influence those people to change. How very wrong I was!

I do love to problem-solve, and I have offered some people some tremendous solutions over the years, only to be surprised by their inability to receive my generous offers of advice. I remember visiting a friend's house in my early twenties and seeing that it had been renovated in a particularly poor fashion. The renovation would need to be maintained regularly because of the nature of the refurbishment. I felt the need to let them know how they could have done the renovation better. I made a good job of criticising their workmanship, and in so in doing so I inadvertently criticised my friend's most significant possession and something that he was very proud of. Rather than coming across as helpful, I came across as arrogant and insensitive, and it is unsurprising that my friend rarely sought my advice (or even my company) thereafter. When we value our own opinion over our connection with others, our relationships inevitably suffer. When we lose connection with others, we lose our ability to positively influence them.

Over the years, I have formulated a saying; "Unsolicited advice is seldom heeded." I could improve that quote now by saying ***"Unsolicited advice is seldom appreciated, let alone heeded!"*** Not only is unsolicited advice seldom followed, but if people aren't asking for advice they generally don't appreciate it being given without invitation. The problem is that advice often comes across as criticism, and nobody ever enjoys being criticised. It makes sense when people react poorly to a negative or critical attitude in which unsolicited advice is delivered. They are not reacting to the information, they are reacting to the negativity.

In the previous story I thought management were my biggest enemy, whereas I realised over time, and with the assistance of a good friend, that my negative attitude was in fact my biggest enemy. At the time, I didn't understand that my attitude was working against my ability to have harmonious relationships - and that I was the one who was suffering more than anyone else because of this. When management made the decision to dismiss all staff and have us reapply for our jobs I was able to change my ***behaviour*** by being more compliant but I hadn't really shifted my ***attitude***. Sometimes a shift in behaviour is enough to cause the attitude to shift along with it, but where people are passive-aggressive in their approach, behavioural change may not necessarily be reflective of attitudinal change. It wasn't until I was challenged with the very menial task that I could actually see that my attitude was causing me to be stuck.

Negativity, combined with a sense of superiority or contempt, is a toxic combination for turning people off to what I have to say. If I approach people with a positive frame of mind that is considerate to their needs as well as my own, I know that I have a much greater chance of getting a constructive outcome than if I approach them with a negative and critical mindset. A positive attitude and a sensitivity to others is foundational to your ability to influence them for good.

CHAPTER TWO

INFLUENCING ABOVE THE LINE

"The price of greatness is responsibility."
Winston Churchill

INTRODUCTION

When we are presented with an issue or a problem that we are required to take responsibility for, we have the choice to either respond 'Above the Line' or 'Below the Line'. These terms were popularized in the book, *The Oz Principle*, written by Connors, Smith and Hickman. The term 'Responding Below the Line' means responding in ways that are more likely to be knee-jerk reactions rather than carefully considered actions. 'Above the Line' responses tend to be less reactionary and are more likely to be thoughtful and considered.

ABOVE AND BELOW THE LINE RESPONSES

'Below the Line' responses commonly include; ***blaming others, making excuses, denying there is an issue, deflecting, derailing, and ultimately avoiding or even overtly failing to take responsibility***. Defensiveness is a key 'Below the Line' response. It is an emotional response that often manifests itself in our body language, our tone of voice, and the actual words we respond with. Unfortunately, defensive responses will always cause the issue to grow and increase in complexity, leaving the recipient with an even bigger problem than they first reacted to. Ultimately, "Below the Line" reactions diminish trust in relationships.

'Above the Line' responses are the antithesis of their 'Below the Line' counterparts: rather than denial - there is an openness that leads to a full awareness of the issue being presented. The key aspect of 'Above the Line' thinking and behavior is the recipient taking responsibility and ownership for resolving the problem rather than blaming others, or getting defensive in some way.

When we are dealing with a problem that requires our ownership in order to see a resolution to that problem, (in other words, it is ***our*** problem), we need first to become ***aware*** of the problem. The leap from 'awareness of the issue' to 'ownership of the issue' is a significant one and tends to require that people use the stepping stones of 'acknowledgement' and 'acceptance' - ***acknowledging*** that there is a real issue to be responded to, and ***accepting*** that ownership will be the key factor in change. Naturally it's not enough simply to verbally take responsibility, we need to walk the talk and come up with an active solution or response that will at least cause the issue to diminish in intensity, if not resolve completely. This kind of response builds trust in relationships.

Reading Between (and Above) the Lines

Many years ago, I was working in a business in which I had a friendship with the senior manager in charge of key accounts. An internal email was circulated concerning a meeting that several us needed to attend regarding a certain client. I was managing a team at the time and in classic, playful Glen Sharkey fashion, I sent a 'reply all' email that included humorous comments to a fellow manager. The senior manager became concerned about my humorous comment given that it appeared that I had copied in the external client by hitting 'reply all'. I received a voicemail message in which the senior manager expressed her concern at the inappropriateness of my humor given this assumption.

I had to work hard in this situation against feeling defensive. But I recognized my 'below the line' reaction immediately and worked hard to counter it. I acknowledged that the Senior Manager had a genuine issue, accepted her perspective, and ultimately took as much ownership for resolving the issue as I possibly could. I phoned her back as soon as possible and accepted that there was room in my communication to be more professional than I had been. I then offered to email all the staff concerned and apologize for my flippancy and said I was also happy to apologize to the staff face-to-face when we came together for our meeting.

When I talk about this scenario in my training I ask participants: "What do you think my senior manager's response was?" More often than not someone will volunteer the answer; "She told you not to worry about it", which is exactly what happened. My manager had been perturbed by my email, but because I so quickly and clearly accepted responsibility for the issue she felt no further course of action was required.

Here's the fascinating aspect of this story: the manager's main concern was that I had copied in the external client when I hit 'reply all', and this client would then have read my humorous 'in-house' comments. However, I hadn't copied in the eternal client at all! When I hit the 'reply all' button, I deleted his address from the email so that it ultimately was only sent internally. So why didn't I stick up for myself and tell my senior account manager that there was really nothing to worry about at all, and she had no grounds for being concerned? Because rather than having an unconsidered reaction, I stopped and thought to myself; "This seems like a strong reaction given the circumstances – so what might be going on here between the lines?" On reflection, I realized that the manager had probably had a concern about the professionalism of my communication for some time, and that this email to (apparently) an external client had tipped the scales for her and caused her to voice her unease. I believe the actual issue was my tone of communication in general. When I responded to that and took ownership for it, she was more than happy for me not to have to do anything further because *I'd acknowledged, accepted, and taken responsibility* for the real issue.

This ultimately put her at ease and her concerns rapidly diminished. She felt heard and acknowledged regarding a real issue in her own mind. It was really about her, rather than the client, so it still required a response from me. 'Below the Line' reactions would have impaired our relationship, but because I chose to respond 'Above the Line', her trust in me increased through this episode.

Ironically, *in being prepared to accept her influence about my manner, and acknowledging her perspective, I gained a greater ability to influence her* and our relationship continued in a stronger fashion. Influence is mutual - it is two way. When we accept the influence of others trust is created which opens the door for others to accept our influence.

A Sorry State of Affairs

Sometime ago I was in a leadership position and I had handed over an area of responsibility to one of my team members. She had always had an issue with punctuality and this new area of responsibility did nothing to change that. On one occasion, I needed to cover for her because of her tardiness. After the event, I took her aside and we had a quiet chat. I made a complaint to her about her ongoing tardiness. She was apologetic, as she always was, but failed to really listen to my complaint, acting in a closed off manner towards me.

When I found out that she didn't have a good reason for being late I said to her, "I think I know what the issue is here - you just don't care about the people you are holding up because of your lateness." She was absolutely irritated by this comment and flatly denied that that was the case. My team leader was a university graduate and so I asked her if she had ever been late for a university exam. She replied that she had not. I then went on to say to her that she had never been late for an exam because she cared enough about herself, and about the way that passing the exam would affect her future, to make sure that she could get to the exam on time. Until she acknowledged that her tardiness showed she didn't care enough about the people she was managing, she wouldn't seriously consider the need to change her behavior. This was a shocking revelation for this person because she considered herself to be very caring, but she wasn't at all aware that in this circumstance her lack of punctuality and preparedness clearly communicated a different message to the people she was managing.

I was never going to have any influence on this person's lack of punctuality while she was in denial as to how she actually felt about the people she was managing. It was necessary to share with her the harsh reality that she was disrespecting those people, to help her get to a place of *acknowledgement and awareness* of the issue and its key causal factors. Only then would I have any chance of influencing her to take ownership for her punctuality.

Come on Up - The View is Spectacular!!

I had a team leader on my course speak to me a few years back regarding one of his team members who he found incredibly frustrating to deal with. Whenever he would sit the person down for a one-on-one conversation about their behavior and their attitude, he felt they side-lined his concern and deflected from the issue he was trying to raise with them. The team leader would find himself getting more and more wound up to the point where he could no longer speak to the person.

I asked him for more details regarding what the person was doing that made it so difficult for him to remain calm. He replied that he struggled to keep the conversation on track because the team member's responses were typically *defensive*. They engaged in a lot of *blame shifting* and attempting to *deflect* the issue on to other teams. The team member would argue that the behavior they were now being pulled up for was being consistently demonstrated by members of other teams. This would cause the team leader to become derailed from focusing on the real issue at hand and instead go into a lengthy discussion regarding the issues that the team member raised about other people's behavior. That was until I made the team leader aware of his defensive team member's clever strategy .

I asked the team leader why he thought that this team member was responding in such a fashion - what did he think their goal was? The leader replied that his team member believed that they were being treated unfairly when people on other teams got away with similar actions, so he thought their goal was to expose a flaw in the company's people management. I explained that the team member's real goal was actually to *avoid* taking ownership and to walk out of the meeting without having to do anything in terms of changing their own behavior or attitude. Their goal was the exact opposite of what the team leader required, which was taking ownership of the problem and ownership of the subsequent solution. Their strategy was very clear regardless of whether it was conscious or subconscious: to deflect the conversation away from the need for them to make any personal changes.

I then discussed with the team leader the strategy that he needed to have to keep the conversation on track, and to remain calm and in control. This required that he *not engage in matters that were irrelevant to their discussion*, and that each time the team member attempted this strategy the team leader was required to calmly and briefly dismiss the deflection and come back to the core issue.

Several weeks later I met up again with the team leader for leadership training and asked how his relationship with his 'challenging' team member was going. He responded that there had been an amazing turnaround! He said that when he remained calm and kept bringing the conversation quickly back on track, despite the team member's attempts to deflect blame and responsibility, it was like a tire being slowly deflated. The strategies that had worked previously for the team member were no longer working and they were now forced to face the core issue on the table in front of them. This demanded that they focus on addressing their own behavior and attitude.

This was a real win-win for the team leader, because not only did he learn that he can shift someone from lacking responsibility to owning a situation, but he also realized that he could do it whilst remaining calm and in control, which is a vital attribute of effective leadership and important in the ability to influence others over the long-term.

When Will I Ever Learn?

A couple of years ago, I was working on the manuscript for my first book and I thought to myself, "What would my teachers think if they could see me now?!" My personal story is not quite one of 'rags to riches', but it is most certainly one of 'unconstructive school room distractor to focused author and award winning educator' (well, sufficiently focused anyway!) I was kicked out of class even from pre-school days, for my constant talking and distracting behavior. I got through Year 12 English by reading the comic and movie versions of Shakespeare! Yet here I was, writing my third book, educating people for a living, and having recently won "The Educator of the Year" for the National Speakers Association of New Zealand .

I was clearly an obnoxious pupil throughout my schooling years and now as an adult I was teaching others. This journey has reshaped my values to taking ownership and responsibility for my attitude and behavior. I realized, as I thought about how far I had come since my school days, that I had never formally taken responsibility for my irresponsible behavior and attitude despite the way they must have negatively affected each one of my teachers. So, I took it upon myself to write a letter of *apology* to my teachers, both for my behavior and my poor attitude, particularly towards what I deemed to be the 'softer subjects' (and therefore, in my opinion, the 'waste

'waste of time subjects') such as English. What I found most con-
victing was that if I had not attended school at all I would certainly
not have been able to read and write and go on to complete several
tertiary qualifications, nor would I have had the ability or the confidence to produce my own books.

In addition to apologizing, I really wanted to encourage the
English teachers that although some of their most difficult pupils
seemed unable to get anything out of their subject, it was clear that I
must have derived some value from them to have gone on with the
confidence that I had regarding the English language.

I sent the letter off to the Principal of my old school. He found
it an encouraging letter and read it out to staff prior to the school
year starting. I'm pleased to say that the staff also found it an encouragement for what can be a very thankless task at times, but for
me it was primarily an opportunity to act 'Above the Line' and take
responsibility for a very irresponsible time in my formative years.

These Boots were Made for Licking!!

Richard Branson is both Britain's entrepreneur of the decade and is
also renown for being something of a 'loose cannon', at least in his
earlier days. He tells the story of being invited to be part of the team
attempting to break the world record for the fastest speedboat crossing of the Atlantic Ocean. Having accepted the invitation, he began
to make enquiries regarding fuel sponsorship and managed to secure
a generous offer from a major petroleum company, British Petroleum (BP).

Branson was called in to meet the members of the BP board,

and as part of his presentation he began to thank BP for their willingness to be involved in the venture. He was somewhat surprised when
the executives sat there in front of him unengaged, yet he proceeded
to express his gratitude and informed them that this world record
attempt would not be possible without the generous sponsorship of
BP.

At this point the members of the leadership team sitting
around the board table became decidedly cold and almost antagonistic towards Branson, and the unimaginable finally dawned on him as
he glanced up at the wall and realized that the petroleum company
that he had been acknowledging and showing gratitude towards was
in actual fact the competitor of the company whose board he was
addressing! He had used the wrong name in his entire presentation!
Horrified by his own unforgivable mistake, he then did what only
Richard Branson would think to do - he dropped to his knees,
crawled under the board table and as he articulated his deepest and
sincerest apologies, he began licking the shoes of the executives
around the table. The final outcome from this courageous action was
that the members of the board were able to graciously accept his
apology and decided not to withdraw their offer of funding the fuel
for his world record attempt!

This is such a wonderful story of Sir Richard Branson *facing a horrible, self-authored 'issue' but taking extreme action to
accept responsibility for his problem.* He did whatever was necessary to take ownership and make the issue de-escalate. In doing so
he was able to influence the directors back into the project when they
had been all but lost to the cause.

THE FOUR CRITICAL FACTORS

Dr John Gottman is one of the world's leading relationship experts. Through his extensive research, he has identified four key factors leading to marriage breakdown. He has defined these four factors as being: criticism, defensiveness, contempt, and withdrawal. When all four horsemen are present in an interaction, both parties have all but lost the ability to take, or have influence over, the other. When these factors are present in interactions in an ongoing manner, inevitably the marriage relationship breaks down completely.

Obviously, the work that I do in the business world does not require me to teach on marriage, but people are people, and their intimate relationship styles affect their working relationships in a similar way. These four factors - criticism, defensiveness, contempt, and withdrawal - are classic 'Below the Line' responses. As leaders, we are looking for the positive workplace correlations to these four corroding factors. We are looking for the 'Above the Line' responses.

The constructive alternative to the first factor - **_harsh criticism_** or personal attack - is to raise the issue in a manner where the person's dignity is respected but where the problematic behavior or attitude is very clearly addressed. Whereas harsh criticism is likely to lead to an unconstructive defensive response, the genuine raising of an issue in a respectful manner is much more likely to solicit an open response. This is deemed a **_complaint_**, as opposed to a criticism.

Issues in the workplace need to be addressed and not swept under the carpet where they can fester and grow, but taking the personal criticism out of the complaint means the hearer is just having to deal with the problem at hand, and not having to defend their personal value and self-esteem as well.

The second negative factor - ***defensiveness*** - is possibly the most unhelpful response in workplace relationships. The line between a criticism and a complaint may be hazy at times, but people are always clear on what a defensive response is. Some people have set up defensiveness as their 'modus operandi', perhaps because of repeated life experiences where they have been put down and criticized as a norm of human interaction. Often these people find it difficult to identify their own negativity. It is easily identified by others though by asking this question: is this person open to taking influence from others? The positive corollary to defensiveness is for the recipient to be open to feedback – open to taking influence.

Ongoing defensiveness eventually leads to the third negative factor – ***contempt***. The constructive opposite to contempt is mutual respect – both shown by the person raising the issue, and on the part of the person whose behavior is being addressed. Contempt is an attitude that may develop when a person has had a past of regular criticism that they have responded to with defensiveness. Over time, to protect their ego from seeming constant attack, they raise their ego up above anyone who attacks them. They begin to look at 'attackers' as people not worth listening to as a way of protecting themselves from having to become vulnerable to their words. An attitude of contempt is generally a poor means of self-protection. Unfortunately, it shuts down the relationship and the taking of influence. Contempt is therefore toxic to all relationships.

If things get to the fourth stage of shut down – ***withdrawal*** and stonewalling - then the relationship has deteriorated to the point where it is almost unsalvageable. This is where people who work together or who have some working relationship start to ignore phone calls, emails, and in the very worst cases literally each other in face-to-face encounters. The constructive opposite to stonewalling is for both parties to remain engaged and to begin the difficult but worthwhile process of being open to the initial issue that was raised. The masters at this work hard to keep communication going, aiming to work out a win-win solution for both parties.

Spiraling Up

I had a leader on my course who inherited a severely dysfunctional team. The team was so far down the 'spiral of doom' that two of the four members had completely withdrawn from each other. Despite working together on a daily basis in the same office they were no longer talking or engaging together. They were genuine 'enemies'. It was so bad that if one of them went to collect the mail they would collect everyone else's - except the 'enemy's'. If one went to get coffee for everyone they would refuse to get it for the 'enemy'.

The leader who had inherited this dysfunctional team came

to me desperate for help with how to get them out of this negative spiral and back into a functioning state. She was a shy person herself and up to this point had not done anything to curb the behavior. My first piece of advice to her was: "DO SOMETHING!" When we allow poor behavior to continue unchecked we are simply agreeing with the one perpetuating the behavior that it is acceptable within our team. She was the leader – she was responsible for deciding the culture of her team.

What we allow or disallow determines the culture that will be created. So, in the first instance the team leader had to re-engage the pair in a conversation. If people refuse to engage together there are only two choices if you want to develop a healthy, enjoyable and sustainable team culture: someone needs to go, or both parties need to begin to communicate again.

Once she had re-engaged the pair, she could then begin to work on reversing the downward spiral they had gotten themselves into. No doubt it was brought about by: criticism, defensiveness, contempt and ultimately withdrawal. To reverse it they would need to reverse these behaviors with ***engagement, respect, openness and non-judgmental conversation.***

Restoring a relationship that has become this damaged in the workplace is not always a simple task. Both parties need to be willing to do the hard work of mending the broken fences. It is up to them, prompted by their leader, to make it work. Both parties need to have the humility to own their part in the damage – and this is not always a 50:50 equation - so both parties need to have the grace to allow for an imperfect process with an imperfect person.

It is completely possible to restore such a broken relationship, but generally only when those conditions are mutually met. If one party isn't willing, then it may be more effective to remove one of the parties from your team. This is what the team leader in the previous anecdote eventually had to do, and it resulted in a great leap forward for her in team productivity and morale. Her responsibility was not to resolve their differences for them, but it was certainly to take back control over her team culture and redefine it according to her own plan, rather than theirs.

CHAPTER THREE

CONNECTING WITH OTHERS

"I've learned that people will forget what you said,
people will forget what you did,
but people will never forget
how you made them feel."
Maya Angelou

INTRODUCTION

People have an inherent need to connect with others. Connecting with others is both the road and the vehicle for influence. When we attempt to influence people without sufficient connection, we do so at our own peril. Connection involves trust. We are unlikely to connect well with people who we don't trust. In fact, we are much more likely to *avoid* connecting with people we don't trust. When I build trust with a person and therefore connect well with them, my influence with them increases, and their influence with me increases, and the connection becomes a wholesome and holistic experience for all involved.

Definitions for the word 'connect' and 'connection' include words and phrases such as: to unite or bind, and to establish communication between. It is possible to influence people without a sense of connection to them, but even if we are able to achieve results without connection, the outcomes are likely to be far less powerful and require much more effort.

3.1

THE MIGHTY FORCE OF CONNECTION

My role as a training facilitator is to deliver informational content, but if you were to ask my various clients what they are really hoping for, many of them would answer that they would love to see *transformational change* in their staff, or words to that effect. In my opinion the key element to achieving this is *through connection* with my audience.

If I don't have connection with people, then I have almost no foundation for having any significant influence in their work or their personal lives. That is why I work so hard so early in every training program that I deliver to discover as many points of connection with as many people as possible. I arrive well before the course day begins, especially on day one of an extended course, and while I'm setting up prior to the day officially starting, I've already begun forming relationships with one, two, or even three people. I know which ones these are because we're chatting away and laughing as if we have been friends for some time.

I've come to describe these people as 'Gateway People'. These are people who are very open to me early on the first day, and who I've connected well with almost immediately. They are on the left-hand side of the 'Early Adopters' bell curve which, according to marketing theory, mean they are the innovators, or those who are very open to change. It's the *'Gateway People'* that allow me much easier access to the trust of others in the group. When the less open 'others' see that I already have a relationship with one or several people in the group prior to the start of the day, this helps them to become open to my influence more readily.

Over the years, I've noticed that at some point, generally on the first day, the group as a whole embraces me as 'one of them'. At this point it's much easier for me to influence the whole group because I've become an 'insider'. This early 'embrace' generally happens as a result of my efforts to connect as soon as possible with the 'Gateway People'. I've found in every group situation where you have a responsibility to influence the group, that genuine connection with a few will foster greater connection with the whole.

Not Quite Scott Free

Many years ago, I started to work with a new client who had centers in several cities around New Zealand. I'm from Auckland which is the largest city in New Zealand. Aucklanders are 'affectionately' known around the country as "JAFA's", which stands for "Just Another F@*#ing Aucklander!" It is somewhat tongue in cheek, but there are certainly pockets of people who believe Auckland has 'large city syndrome' and out of this perception has grown a type of 'city-ism' (racism based on city of residence).

I had flown into Dunedin city - one of New Zealand's southernmost cities. On the lengthy drive from the airport to my hotel I began to ponder the issue of how to best connect with my new training attendees and overcome 'JAFAism'. As I began to think about any connections that I may have to Dunedin it occurred to me that it's known as the most Scottish of all the cities of New Zealand, having had a sizeable Scottish population of early settlers who pioneered the area. I am half Scottish on my father's side, although I can't admit to feeling it all that strongly, not having known him for longer than a few months of my life.

I am working with countless new groups every year and *I prioritize getting to know my groups, and letting them get to know me,* so at the start of every new course. I show a slideshow of photos to add a visual aspect to my personal introduction to new groups. At the end of my short slideshow I talk about various aspects of my life. The final image in my slideshow is a black-and-white photograph of a jockey. I ask the attendees who they think the photo is of, and generally, because of the similarities of looks, one of the participants will volunteer the answer that it is my father.

In Dunedin I was training a safety leadership course, but

some of the participants were not specifically leading teams of people. I invariably have the issue of participants in my training who don't have any direct reports. They question why they are on a leadership program when they aren't actually leading anyone. In these scenarios, I focus on the concept of influence, rather than leadership. Every one of my attendees has influence over others, regardless of if it is with a formal team of staff members. On this day in Dunedin I used the story of my father's early death to talk about how he could potentially still be alive if someone had made the effort to influence him not to drink and drive on that fateful night some five decades ago, where a drink-drive accident took his life. It is a poignant reminder of the powerful positive reason we should cultivate our influence skills for the good of other's life outcomes.

Room for Improvement

I once had a gentleman at the conclusion of a day's training who lingered in the room. I know by now that this is usually an indication that they want to talk to me about a personal matter. Sure enough, this gentleman wanted to ask me how he should deal with his university age son. He was very pleased with his son's diligence with his university work. However, the father was frustrated by his own inability to influence his son to perform household chores, and in particular to make any headway whatsoever with his 'bombsite' of a bedroom.

I started by quizzing the father on the current state of his relationship with his son and when I found out that it was quite strained, I explained that I didn't think he had sufficient relational 'money in the bank' to successfully address the issue of the boy's bedroom. I told him I was concerned that if he continued to push his son in terms of tidiness then their relationship was in danger of going into overdraft. Instead I suggested that he work on putting some significant deposits into their 'relational account' with activities, like taking his son away for a weekend, spending time in conversation with him and about him, and trying to respond to him with openness rather than with criticism, or contempt. Once their account was in a healthy state, then he would likely have more success addressing the son's orderliness in a way that was more likely to influence his behavior, rather than put further stress on an already strained relationship.

This father was attempting to achieve influence with insufficient connection with his son, and as a result he was shutting his son down and achieving the opposite of what he was hoping for. He had every right to be concerned about his son's lack of orderliness, but in some situations, it is necessary to work on connection before influence can be achieved - and this was certainly one of those. The importance of connection correlates directly to the length and depth of the relationship. The longer and more important the relationship, the more critical becomes the issue of connection in relation to achieving positive and lasting influence.

Very Sorry to Say

I have been in training roles for most of my work life, starting with a decade of working with young, unemployed people. I dipped my toes into the public education system for a couple of years, and spent several years in charitable organizations in leadership roles. When I began to transition back into corporate training I had a significant skill set but that doesn't always equate to confidence, and for my first few training programs I was a little on edge and not nearly as comfortable as I am now.

On one occasion in those early days I was delivering core work skills training to operators in a manufacturing business. These were short, two-hour sessions which involved seven groups in total. I was just about to take the first session for a new group when a gentleman came walking up to me in his overalls and said in a gruff and terse manner, "Are you the guy that I complain to about being in this course?" I felt like saying to him, "I'm good thanks, how are you?", but I'm pleased to say I didn't! I explained to him that it wasn't really my place to decide who attended the program and who didn't, but I spent some time listening to his opinion that the training was not worthwhile given that he was in his last year of employment prior to retirement. Finally, I said to him, "This training is only for a couple of hours so if you can agree to stay for this session then I'll give you the fortnight in between this session and the next to get permission from management to be withdrawn from the program." I was marginally confident that he might change his mind once he'd participated in my program. He reluctantly agreed. Even though the session was only two hours long, I still knew it was important to get to know the people I was training. This was no exception. When this gentleman introduced himself to the group, he talked about his history with the company and about how resentful he was towards it. When I queried him as to why that was the case he told us his daughter had worked at the company also and she had miscarried her first child, his first grandchild. In his opinion this was because of constant exposure to toxic chemicals in the manufacturing process. As you can imagine I was touched by his grief over the loss of his grandchild. I talked to him individually at the end of the session and thanked him for his honesty.

Although I made no attempt to encourage him to return to the training (we had made a deal which I intended to stick to), his closing remarks on leaving that day were that he would see me in a couple of weeks' time. Over the seven sessions that he attended, he shifted from being one of the least willing participants on the program to one of its biggest advocates, suggesting to many of his colleagues that they should attend too. I would never have had this gentleman continue the course, let alone become one of its greatest proponents, if I hadn't made such a meaningful connection with him and his 'point of pain' in the first session. On this occasion connection was absolutely crucial if I was to have any chance of influencing him to stay and be open to the course content.

3.2

THE BRIDGE OF INQUISITIVENESS

Although there is significant overlap between being inquisitive and caring for people, they are not the same - but they make worthy partners in terms of influencing people and situations. It is possible to be incredibly caring for people and not articulate that care for all manner of honorable and not so honorable motives. Of course, there are times when to be inquisitive and to curiously dig a little deeper to better understand someone's circumstances would be highly inappropriate and amount to a serious invasion of privacy. However, in my experience those times are few and far between, and even if your enquiry is rejected, the person often still appreciates your query if your ***motive is a genuine interest*** in their life and well-being.

I am constantly working with people for the first time, and the longest relationship I would have with them in terms of program length is only eight days, spread over as long as eight months. Even in these programs I still tend to spend a maximum of two days in a row with any group at any time. I'm relating to people as members of groups of up to 15 people, so my ability to spend one-on-one time with anyone is limited. Despite this apparent lack of relationship, people will reveal areas of their personal and professional lives to me because firstly they sense that I care, and secondly, I'm very confident to be quite inquisitive, so I'll often ask the questions that others in the same position might be very hesitant to ask.

Them's Fighting Words

I was administering some pre-course assessments to a group that I would be training several weeks later. These assessments are quite clinical and require me to simply hand them out and monitor any questions that the learners may have as they silently complete them.

As the participants walked into the room I introduced myself to each one in turn, shook their hands and asked them their names. They then sat down and I handed them the assessments.

As I handed the last one out I could see that one recipient had a scuff mark above his cheek. Not being one to hold back I asked him, somewhat tongue and cheek at the time, if he had been in a fight. I was genuinely surprised when he replied that indeed he had been. Because it was early in the morning I wondered if he had had a fight with a fellow staff member so I asked him when the fight had occurred and what it had been over. He replied that the fight occurred the night before at a friend's funeral. Both curiosity and empathy rose in me and I asked him why there had been a fight at the funeral. At this point I was quite taken aback by his reply: he said the fight had been started by attendees at the funeral who were supportive of the man who had murdered his friend. Naturally quite a conversation occurred following this disclosure.

Although I was only giving out and supervising the assessments, I couldn't help but want to connect more with the young man. He went on to tell me that his friend had been stabbed to death in an altercation at a party and that the killer had been only sentenced to assault because of his young age. This is a horrific incident for this young man to have been party to and I was so pleased that I was made aware of the tragedy so early on. I was certainly keen to process this tragedy with him throughout the course and could tell that it would be the most significant way I could support his training journey into the future.

I guess I had three options when I first saw the mark on his face. Firstly, I could have ignored it, but I have an inquisitive nature and I love to hear people's stories. Secondly, I could have chosen to ask him what the mark on his face was, which would have been a softer option and given him the chance to potentially fabricate a story that would have meant he could avoid telling me the truth. But it's my nature to cut straight to the heart of a matter and so without thinking I chose a third option and asked him if he'd been in a fight. Because of the accuracy of that question it may have disarmed any consideration he might have had of not telling me the truth about what had happened. I'm certainly glad that I asked the question and I'm really glad that he answered honestly and openly.

I've learnt to push the boundaries of how far I can go with inquisitiveness by, not surprisingly, respectfully pushing the boundaries of inquiry. I'm happy to keep asking more and more in-depth questions and leaving the 'that's far enough' decision up to the other party, rather than me making assumptions on their behalf and having a less productive conversation and less connection as a result. My inquisitiveness is the vehicle that my care is often transported in and together they open the doors for meaningful relationship and the chance, if necessary and appropriate, for positive influence.

Get on Board!!

I was asked recently if I ever work with people who, for whatever reason, are unable to, or refuse to, change. My reply was that of the hundreds of people that I work with each year I may have two or three that I'm unable to shift. This is usually because I struggle to connect with them. ***Connecting with people in order to bring about a genuine attitudinal shift is absolutely paramount.***

Some time ago I was working with a group of learners who were facing the possibility of redundancy and the complete closure of their business for the first time in over 100 years. This training was a little unusual for me as I was filling in for only one day for another training colleague who was unwell. This trainer had already bonded with the group after several days training with them. I was therefore on the back foot from the start - and not only because I was filling in for a fellow facilitator - but also because he was from a similar geographic region as those he was training, whereas I had flown in from Auckland - the city of JAFA's.

One of the participants was particularly negative and was not shifting in a hurry. Given that I only had one day to work with them it could have been very easy for me just to have tolerated his negativity, but it really concerned me because it was impacting on the rest of the group. So, I got all the attendees to introduce themselves to me, as I would if I was starting out fresh with a course of my own. Even though it was only a one-day relieving job I still wanted to get to know them and let them get to know me.

When the negative attendee introduced himself, he mentioned that he had been spending his free time at home working on restoring a recreational vehicle, a bus, and when I found out that he had come to training in his bus that day I asked him if I could have a look at it at morning break. It wasn't my intention at all to use this as a ploy to shift his negativity. I have done a lot of house renovating, and one of my main hobbies is furniture building, and I have even renovated an old caravan myself in the past, so I was genuinely interested to see what he had done and was in the process of doing with his bus.

Several of the group ended up marching out to the vehicle during the break and we spent a fair bit of time looking through it with him - admiring some of the features that he had built and some of the bespoke pieces he had made. I was particularly fascinated by a copper kettle that he had crafted and soldered together - it was a real work of art. I talked to him about some of the background story to the bus, including how he had gone about purchasing it and getting it road legal. It wasn't an overtly animated conversation for anyone observing us, but the change when he got back to the room was a 180-degree shift in his attitude. Not only did he start to communicate much more positively, he also started to pull others up for being negative - a dramatic change - and all because I'd taken a genuine interest in something that was a huge personal investment of his time, money, and creativity – something genuinely important to him.

Now You're Talking

I remember discussing this concept of inquisitiveness and curiosity with a group of people in one of my leadership programs. A couple of the participants stated that they would never be so inquisitive with their team members, and they also would not appreciate people enquiring to any significant depth about their personal lives either. One of the participants said that he had gone through a particularly rough personal patch recently and he would certainly not be willing or happy to talk about this with anyone else. He said it was very personal and he saw no productive end in sharing it with others. I respected his opinion and appreciated his clear boundary and we moved on with the course content.

At the conclusion of the day I bumped into the same participant in the carpark as I was leaving. As we were on our own I checked with him to see if he was OK after the earlier conversation. I apologized to him if I'd embarrassed him or come across as invasive in any way. He then proceeded to talk to me for the next half hour in detail about just what he'd been going through personally. I was able to give him some useful advice and encouragement and I believe he felt a degree of relief in discussing the issue with me. This illustrates the fact that even people who claim not to appreciate others being inquisitive may actually be objecting to something else, such as the inappropriate timing, or the venue for the inquiry. Ultimately *the clear majority of people want to have others take an interest in them,* even if they come across as somewhat guarded initially.

It is an innate part of the human psyche to want to be known by others. Some are more than willing to divulge the inner workings of their personal worlds (and sometimes offer far too much information) and some at the opposite end of the spectrum do not respond well to what feels to them to be prying nosiness. But both the latter and the former are few and far between and after 30 years of working with thousands of people, many of whom I've had very little re-lationship with in the bigger scheme of things, I've learnt that people appreciate your taking a genuine interest in their lives.

We generally err on the side of being far too cautious when it comes to showing an interest in other people's worlds. As a result, we miss so many valuable opportunities to connect, and at the same time to increase our understanding and awareness of others. When demonstrating consideration for others by being inquisitive we also dramatically increase our chances of having a positive influence in people's lives.

Reading His ~~Mind~~ Head

I was training in another city, and when I'm out of town I try to get to a local gym to keep my fitness regime on track. Towards the end of my workout I noticed a man on the far side of the gym with a shaved head and a huge swastika tattooed on the side of it. I'm not at all a fan of Nazism and on several occasions I've freely spoken out against racism even in a public setting, but I was really intrigued as to what type of person would be so committed to an ideology that they would tattoo themselves in such a prominent position with such a universally antagonistic symbol. I was so intrigued that I really wanted to go over and talk to him even though he was obviously training with a friend. I could hear voices inside my head saying, "Leave him alone and mind your own business." But my curiosity got the better of me and I found myself walking over to the part of the gym where he and his friend were working out and striking up a conversation with them both.

Now to be honest what I would have liked to have told him would be that he was wrong in his thinking and he should listen to my opinions about swastikas and Nazism so that he could get his thinking right. That certainly would have been the tack that I might have taken 20 or so years ago. But instead I sat down on an incline sit up bench, putting me at a much lower eye level than this pair, and in effect coming to him as a learner and not a lecturer.

I began by saying that it was none of my business and he should feel free to tell me so if he wanted to, but I was really interested in what the tattoo on his head meant (no point beating around the bush). I could see that he tensed up slightly and was assuming a defensive standpoint that he had no doubt adopted many times previously. He answered my question with a fairly blunt tone, "It stands for White Power." I explained to him that I didn't want to appear smart but that I honestly didn't know what he meant by 'White Power', which in all honesty was true. I had some assumptions about what it meant, but I had never conversed before with someone who has a more intimate relationship with the words than I do.

The question and *my genuine tone seemed to de-escalate the conversation* slightly, and probably to test me he replied, in somewhat shocking words, that he had a history of bad experiences with 'non-whites' (he used a different 'N' word than 'non-whites'). I think he was quite surprised when I failed to act shocked and didn't take the bait of his racial slur. I simply asked him what kinds of trouble he had had. If I'm honest it would have been my ultimate desire to have shifted his thinking but it was important that I made it a priority to try to understand his journey. I genuinely wanted to know from his perspective how he had arrived at the point where he would voluntarily mark himself with a symbol of that nature.

When he could genuinely see that I was not there to argue against his ideologies he softened considerably and told me some of his story. He was the head of a white supremacy chapter whilst only in his early 20s. He had been imprisoned but it was his intention not to go back to prison and certainly not to end up like his father who was covered in swastikas and had spent most his adult life in prison. So, in fact, the man that I was talking to was doing much better than his father at this point in life.

We had a really good conversation in which I asked him some pretty searching questions, not about his ideas on racism which I think were merely symptomatic, but about his life to this point and about his future. He had very little vision for his future apart from staying out of prison, so my heart went out to him. We all need hope! Because I had made an effort to listen to his story and not be judgmental I was able to say some encouraging things to him about his future in terms of career and relationships - not something that I had intended to do when I first looked across the gym at him, and not something that I was confident I would be able to do unless the conversation had gone really well.

As he was leaving the gym with his friend, I asked him if I could get a selfie with them both. They obliged, and then I asked him to take off his cap and turn his head sideways so I could get the swastika in the shot. It's probably an indication of how well the conversation had gone, and just how confident I felt about the connection we had made in a such a short period of time, that I felt secure in the fact that he wouldn't be offended by my request. I wanted to record the moment for posterity and I think he trusted that I wouldn't misuse the photograph, so he agreed. I've been back to the same gym a couple of times since and haven't seen him, but I keep looking out for him and I look forward to our next encounter where I can continue to engage with him.

When I first spotted this young man, I did have the desire to influence his thinking right from the outset, but at the very least any attempts to do so would have been rebuffed, and worst case scenario I could have come away from the encounter feeling physically sore! This was one of those circumstances in which inquisitiveness not only opened the door to meaningful dialogue where I might be able to have some positive influence, but it also helped me gain an enlarged understanding of the different ways in which people view and process their lives.

It was apparent when I first questioned him that he was very quick to adopt an assertive stand given that he had, no doubt, had plenty of aggressive encounters in his short life. But very quickly he ascertained that I wasn't there to criticize his viewpoint or force mine upon him, and in a short period of time he was quite open with me. The element that was crucial was the manner in which my inquisitiveness manifested itself. It was important that ***I didn't have a critical, or contemptuous tone***, and that my questioning was not merely a means to an end, namely to open him up so that I might impose my ideologies upon him.

I guess Jesus knew a thing or two when He said, "Treat others the way that you would like to be treated." Interestingly, in this

His telling of this lesson He immediately goes on to say, "If you love only those who love you, why should you get credit for that?" It seems that Jesus understood that showing an interest in those that may not return the favor is a real sign of genuine care, and *care is what really counts when it comes to connecting with people and having influence* in their lives.

It's one thing to emotionally care for people but unless that care manifests itself behaviorally somehow, then people either don't know that you care or even worse, doubt that you do. Inquisitiveness is a great way to demonstrate to people that you are interested in them and their perspective. I can be a very caring person but if I don't ask you questions and make enquiries as to your thoughts on various issues, then I may seem as disinterested in you as someone who only talks about themselves.

All Kid(napp)ing Aside

Having trained people from multiple nationalities over the years I have always been fascinated by South Africans and the way they often wholeheartedly embrace their migration to New Zealand as a new homeland. When I meet a South African I'll often enquire as to the reason for their decision to change continents. I regularly get a reply along the lines of: things became too violent in South Africa and family safety became a genuine concern.

I remember talking to a South African immigrant and asking him if he had ever experienced violence first hand. He replied that he hadn't. Then he paused and corrected himself. He remembered an occasion during which he was kidnapped! I was absolutely dumb-

founded that anyone could forget a first-hand case of being kidnapped and when I enquired about that he told me that he never at
any point feared for his well-being so at first it had slipped his mind.
As might be guessed, I had a few questions for him after that, and
regardless of whether it opened a door of influence or not, he really
was a fascinating person to talk to and his story intrigued me.

People tend to appreciate genuine inquisitiveness. It has
been said that peoples' favorite word is their own name, which
means that peoples' favorite subject is also themselves. Most people
want to be asked more questions rather than less, and more people
are willing to open up and share their perspective than there are people willing to ask the questions. In fact, I've been surprised over the
years by just how inquisitive I can be and still not have people rebuff
me for being too personal.

I would rather ask more questions from the point of view of
being genuinely interested, have the person know that I really care,
and then discover at some point that I have come up against a boundary, than err on the side of caution because of my own limiting assumptions. ***When people open up and are vulnerable it causes
greater human connection***, and subsequently greater chance of their
being influenced. As the old saying goes, "People don't care how
much you know until they know how much you care."

Trials and Tribulations

I have adapted an activity in my training where, after introductions, I
ask people, "What is one significant challenge that you have faced in
your life and have overcome?" I tell participants that it is at their

discretion how significant a challenge they choose to share with the group, and that they are welcome to talk about as significant or insignificant a challenge as they like. They are also free to share a challenge that they are going through currently and which they have yet to overcome. The challenge can relate to any area of their lives – not just their work lives. I am astounded at how quickly people open up and share life's challenges with fellow participants that they have only just met. People share about divorce, terminal illness, redundancy, childhood illnesses, health and wellbeing challenges, alcohol overuse, the death of close family members, and everything in between.

I recently ran a two-day leadership program and at the end of the second day one of the participants stated that the highlight of the two days for him was how openly and powerfully people shared their most significant challenges on the morning of day one. ***People are curious about what others have been through*** - that's why gossip magazines sell so well - and why watching reality TV drama has become so popular. But as interesting as people's trials and tribulations are, it's heart-warming to hear about people overcoming adversity. As Napoleon Bonaparte said, "Leaders are dealers in hope", and everyone needs hope! When we share our own stories of dealing with life's problems we help others to know that, firstly, they are not alone in their own difficulties, and secondly, maybe there are ways they too can overcome those same difficulties in their own lives.

Your story of change can throw a pebble in the pond of influence that sends ripples far beyond your own personal reach!

SEEING THINGS FROM THEIR PERSPECTIVE

"I wonder how many people I've looked at
all my life and never seen."
John Steinbeck

INTRODUCTION

People are more open to our influence if they first feel they have been heard and understood. In fact, being heard and understood is a key way people feel cared for, and when people feel cared for, they are much more likely to be open to our influence. When we truly hear what people are saying, it gives us the privilege of entering into their world, and their perspective.

4.1

SEEK FIRST TO UNDERSTAND

Maintaining a humble attitude is important in the quest to understand another person's perspective. We don't ever know everything we need to know, or could know about a person or situation. Often we need to increase our own knowledge of the bigger picture. If we go in guns blazing with our own opinion and our own perspective, we may come away embarrassed when we realize that some of what we thought was fact was only our assumption. It is much safer to attempt to understand the other party's position first, showing them respect and genuine interest, thus paving the way for them to do the same with you.

When dealing with a team member under your supervision regarding their compliance, or lack thereof, to systems and procedures, it is very natural when attempting to influence them to try to be very clear on what it is that *you* want to have happen, but to not be at all cognizant of *their* needs or wants. We are much more likely to have people listen to our position and entertain our opinions on their need for change if we can demonstrate the fact that we understand their position and if we articulate what we believe they will gain by following through on our suggestions.

Questioning the Game Plan

Several years ago, I had the privilege of having the 2011 World Cup All-Black coach - Graham Henry - attend my leadership training as a

79

guest speaker. As part of his presentation to my course on leadership he told a story about Tana Umaga, who was captain of the team at that time. Graham talked about how he had had to adjust his leadership style over the years to get the best out of his young players. At one point Tana approached him and asked if they could catch up for a coffee midweek, which Graham agreed to. As they began to talk Tana asked Graham why he gave speeches to the team on the bus on the way from the hotel to the ground for each international test match. Graham replied that he had always done so and that his intention was to motivate and focus the team. Graham then asked Tana why he was querying him, so Tana openly and honestly said that he and some other members of the team found the talks distracting to the point of being demotivating, and that they would really appreciate it if Graham could desist from those bus talks on the way to the game. Graham agreed to stop doing them and from that day forward never did another team talk on the way to the ground, and instead allowed his players to take that time to focus themselves.

Tana's approach was very skillful in terms of influence because he began by asking Graham to *explain the reason why* he did the talks. Although Tana personally found them unconstructive it may have been that in understanding the bigger picture he would have been prepared to support his coach and conclude that the talks should continue. It was a great example of being open to the influence of someone in authority over you, and that in doing so you increase the chance of them being open to your influence regarding your opinion or perspective. As Stephen Covey so aptly put it: "Seek first to understand." Understanding is the first building block in problem solving and conflict resolution.

4.2

MAY I HELP YOU?

Some time ago I was delivering leadership training, and at separate times during the training the CEO and another member of the senior leadership team popped in to see how things were going. One of the themes that had been brought up during the course that day was how to influence the manager above you, and so I asked them both what they had learnt in terms of 'leading up' over the years. I was fascinated that both these senior leaders had exactly the same response - without any preparation and without having talked to each other - just simply from their decades of experience in business. Both replied that the simplest way to open up a 'leading up' conversation is to say, ***"Help me to understand…?"*** When we start by saying, "Help me to understand…", it communicates to the other party that we are willing to open our ears and our minds to hearing what they have to say. In doing so, we increase our chances of having the other party be open to what we have to say. "Help me to understand" opens up a door of influence.

In the process of trying to understand another person's perspective questions are vital. If we want to become good influencers, we must become good questioners. Effective questioning can be made simpler by remembering these six key question starters: what, when, who, where, how, and why. As Rudyard Kipling once described them: "I keep six honest serving men, they taught me all I knew; their names are 'What' and 'Why' and 'When' and 'How' and 'Where' and 'Who'". Of these six, 'why' is the most likely to take you quickly to

81

the source of motivation, and consequently to a greater depth of understanding of the other person's perspective.

The strength of these six questions is in their opening up of the conversation. They place the responsibility for talking and clarifying with the person you are wanting to understand. This is important because if you truly want to understand someone else's perspective then you need to let them do a lot of talking and you need to do a lot of listening.

IF YOU TRULY WANT TO UNDERSTAND SOMEONE ELSE'S PERSPECTIVE THEN YOU NEED TO LET THEM DO A LOT OF TALKING AND YOU NEED TO DO A LOT OF LISTENING.

4.3

AUTHENTIC LISTENING

It is imperative that we are genuine in our willingness to listen and understand the other party. If this authenticity is **not** present, then your personal agenda and lack of sincerity will become obvious very quickly.

When you ask a question your body language, and in particular, your facial expression, will clearly demonstrate how interested or how disinterested and potentially antagonistic you feel towards the answer. Are you really listening to hear their response? Or are you busy planning your answer while they are still talking?

Genuine listening is evidenced through turning our attention to the speaker in the first instance. When we give someone our attention we look at them. We aren't looking over their shoulder at what is going on behind them, or glancing at our phone to see what new message has come through. We are looking at them and paying attention to their story and their body language.

Once we are giving them our attention – we need to stay engaged in listening. We show that we are still engaged by responding to their comments, and our body language should be mirroring the emotion of the conversation. When the story is funny we might laugh, if it is sad, we might show empathy through a grimace or frown. Whether we like it or not our body language is telling the person whether we are genuinely listening to them or not.

We can't hope to gain another person's perspective without truly hearing what it is. While a lot of our behavior in life is based upon assumption, in this instance, we have to set aside our assumptions and really try to understand how it is to think and feel about a topic from a different life experience and context. When we are prepared to understand someone at this level, it builds a high degree of trust in the relationship.

Pulling the Wool Over Somebody's Goodbye

One of my favorite stories to recall when speaking on the subject of influencing others is the story of the Detmer Woolen Company from Dale Carnegie's all-time bestselling book *How to Win friends and*

Carnegie talks about a customer of the Woolen Company who was so frustrated with being harassed about an outstanding bill that he finally travels to the Woolen Company and tells the Accounts Payable staff, in person, that not only is he absolutely refusing to pay their bill, which he is entirely certain he has already paid, but that he will also never do business with the company again. The owner of the Woolen Company, Julian Detmer, ushers the man into his office and goes to great lengths to **de-escalate** his heightened nature, saying that no doubt his Accounts Payable staff has made a mistake given that they have thousands and thousands of accounts to have to look after while this customer only has one. He **apologizes** for the frustration that his company has caused the customer and eventually invites him out to lunch, which had been their practice when this customer visited the city. The customer reluctantly agreed, and they had such a good lunch that upon their return to the company offices, he placed the largest order that he had ever placed. Not only that, but he returned to his own business in such a better frame of mind that he looked through his accounts and discovered that he had been wrong the whole time and had failed to pay the bill, upon which he promptly paid it. The gentleman remained a loyal customer of the Detmer Woolen Company from that time forward and even gave one of his children the middle name of Detmer!

This is an astounding story of turning someone's attitude around 180°. This customer, who had vowed never to do business with the company again, became completely won over during a lunchtime conversation to the point where they became a lifelong customer.

The story makes me believe that almost anyone can be influenced, even to the point of a polar opposite shift, but that one of the key strategies is first being prepared to see things from the other person's perspective, which Julian Detmer did masterfully. Genuine listening in order to truly hear another's perspective plays a powerful role in the give and take of influence.

CHAPTER FIVE

INFLUENCING TROUBLESOME BEHAVIOR

"The secret of change is to focus all of your energy, not on fighting the old, but on building the new."
Socrates

INTRODUCTION

We know that the vehicle and the road towards influencing others is care, so what are the roadmaps for this journey? How do we conduct ourselves as we navigate through difficult conversations to reach an end result of "win-win"? When dealing with a difficult customer, staff member or situation it helps to have frameworks in mind which can guide you through the process of dialogue to help you reach a safe and positive outcome in a potentially negative situation.

The English have a solution for troublesome situations: a

cup of tea. Had a rough day? A cup of tea will help. Been through a traumatic incident? You need a cup of tea to calm your nerves! While this may seem a little cliché, taking time out for a cup of tea does have some genuinely helpful rationales. Having a cup of tea changes the immediate tone, creates a space of calm, and meets a basic personal need. When we are dealing with a difficult customer, staff member or situation (or all three at once!) we do well to remember these concepts: 1. **Change the tone** (even a small change of environment can help with this – such as sitting down from standing up), 2. **Create a calm space**, and 3. **Try and meet at least one of the needs** that the situation has become troubled over, even if it is a very small personal need, such as simply being heard.

A BISCuit AND A CUP OF TEA

A cup of tea is a good start but a lot of people like to have a biscuit with their cup of tea. My BISCuit Model is a framework that I devised to help give people a clear route when approaching courageous conversations, especially with a team member in the workplace. It is especially useful where you are fearful of the person's response and feel anxious regarding the potentially negative ramifications of addressing the issue with them.

These conversations are called courageous for a reason - we need to overcome our fear of how the other person will or may react. The BISCuit Model acts like a roadmap along a difficult stretch of highway where it would be very easy to slip off the edge and careen down the bank. The BISCuit Model encourages people to plan for these kinds of conversations using the acronym BISC (the first four letters of the word biscuit).

BISC stands for: BEHAVIOR, IMPACT, SHIFT, and - only if necessary - CONSEQUENCES.

5.2

BEHAVIOR

In the kinds of conversations where we are bringing up an issue with someone else and we need to influence them to act or perform in a more desirable fashion than they currently are, it is important to clearly spell out the behavior that is inappropriate or is failing to meet our expectations.

For some of the people you need to address this opening part of the conversation will come as a surprise. They may be completely unaware that their behavior is undesirable. You may need to re-examine how clearly you articulated your expectations of them in the first place. It is best to think this through prior to the conversation happening, but you should at least be prepared to consider it during the interaction. If the person is genuinely surprised, and even some-what disappointed that they have failed to meet expectations, then there is every chance that they are **unclear of those expectations** in the first place. In cases such as these some consideration needs to be given to your role in the unmet expectations.

I do a lot of leadership training that entails the ability to have courageous conversations with team members. It is a common prob-lem (you are not on your own!) and it is worth adding that often these conversations center around an undesirable **attitude** more than an undesirable *behavior*. In regard to influencing attitude, we need to keep the nebulous nature of attitude in mind. Attitude is intangible and unseen whereas behavior is much more visible and invariably is the tangible outworking of attitude. So, when I am addressing someone about an undesirable attitude it is prudent for me to give concrete examples of how that attitude manifests itself as a behavior.

I will ***give them examples of the behaviors that need to cease or diminish, and on the other hand, I will give examples of the kind of behaviors that I need to see more of***. For instance, if I am dealing with a staff member who has a negative attitude then I might talk to them about the kind of behaviors they are displaying that are evidence of this attitude, such as; scoffing at new ideas in meetings or making random comments to upset the momentum of constructive conversations. It is much harder to identify and see attitude change than it is to target tangible behavioural change and it is also clearer for both parties to see progress being made with behavior shift. ***The clearer we can define the change that needs to happen behaviorally, the more likely it is to be changed.***

5.3

IMPACT

Often people who are behaving poorly fail to see the broader impacts of their actions. If the other party is already aware that their behavior is less than adequate, then they may not be so easily influenced to change simply by being told of the offending behavior. If they haven't changed when they already have an awareness and clarity about their poor behavior, then you need to take a step up from simple

about their poor behavior, then you need to take a step up from simple awareness of the issue in resolving it with them. In this case, it may be helpful for them to understand the negative impacts that their behavior is having.

If they do not respond positively and in an engaged fashion when the behavior is challenged then they may actually be unaware of the wider implications (the impact) their behavior is having on concerned parties. *A dialogue around the broader impact of their negative behavior can be enlightening* and helpful to their process of taking influence from you regarding altering their behavior. Some people describe this process as giving people a 'reason big enough' to motivate change.

Detrimental impacts in a workplace setting that people may be unaware of include: the effect the behavior is having on other team members, on other colleagues and peers, on clients and customers, on suppliers and other stakeholders, on the broader company and its reputation, and also on the person's own reputation.

It may also be appropriate to talk about the negative impact that the person's behavior is having on you as their team leader or manager. If undesirable behavior is left to continue unchecked, it sends an inadvertent message to the rest of the team that the behavior is acceptable and therefore lowers the standards of the team. Therefore, it is necessary for

BISC: BEHAVIOR, IMPACT, SHIFT, CONSEQUENCES.

everyone's sake that undesirable behavior and its impacts are addressed as early as possible in these kinds of conversations.

Wood That They Would Change

I worked with one site manager who supervised lumber jacks. When he reached a point of impasse with a resistant staff member he would say to them; "We are not getting anywhere with this, so we will meet again tomorrow morning first thing. In the meantime, go to your locker, grab your gear, go home now, and when your partner asks you why you are home so early you can explain to them why you are risking your future with this company." That strategy almost always returned results, often with people immediately turning their attitude around on the spot! When we think through the broader impact of our behavior on others, it can be revelatory.

5.4

SHIFT

Having talked about the ***behavior*** that is inappropriate, and having covered sufficient elements of the ***impact*** of this behavior, it then becomes necessary to talk about the ***shift*** required. As important as the clarity of expectations is in the process of initially setting the bar for attitude and behavior, the same level of clarity is required in terms of the shift that is needed to resolve poor behavior. It is the task of the person wanting to influence the behavior to make sure that the offending party understands the required shift.

It is not enough for problematic behavior to be addressed, it also needs to *change*. What needs to be eliminated? What needs to be added? What needs adjustment? Make sure both parties are very clear on the nature of the change required, and on how you will both know when that change has occurred. If expectations were lacking in the first instance, then make sure they are crystal clear in this instance. You don't want to have to go around that mountain again! If you are dealing with a staff member, it will probably help to write the expectations down and date and sign them together. Then pin them up in an easily viewable location.

It's the Principal the Counts

Several decades ago while still at school I found myself with some degree of regularity in the headmaster's office for disciplinary action. This would most likely mean five to ten minutes where the head master talked 'at' me, and then in conclusion, would ask me some kind of closed question like; "So are we clear?" or, "Do you understand?" Presumably this was to ascertain whether I understood the error of my ways and what the desired rehabilitated behavior was to be. I often use this in communication training as an example of a poor question choice to establish whether the person has understood the main substance of the conversation, because it does little to clarify that understanding has actually occurred and does nothing to establish that we are 'on the same page'.

In courageous, performance-based conversations it pays to remember that *the person who does the majority of the talking also does the majority of the work*. When my headmaster spent most of his time speaking 'at' me, I was doing very little thinking about my actual behavior and the impact that it had on others. In fact, if he was actually able to see what I was thinking about at the time he would have most likely seen images of a football field or West Coast waves. I was present in body only! The headmaster would have achieved a much more effective result if he had asked me, "So what do you think you need to change?", and not been satisfied with, "I dunno", which would have been my immediate response, not because I didn't know, or couldn't generate an answer, but because I could be confident that that kind of an answer would get him talking again, and I could go back to 'zoning out'.

In terms of having a genuine influence in these kinds of conversations where the recipient is resistant to change, it is a simple but effective strategy to have them talk more, and you less. This is much more likely to happen with persistent questioning, and especially using the open-ended question starters of "what, how, and why?" By having them feedback their behavior, their reasons and rationales for such behavior, what they know or consider to be the impact on others, and what they believe is the desired shift required, you engage them in the process. So remember to get them talking by asking pertinent questions: *1. what they understand the poor behavior or attitude to be; 2. why they think they are behaving like this; 3. how this behavior is affecting others; 4. what they need to change.*

CONSEQUENCES

The first three stages of the BISC Model - explaining the undesirable *behavior*, the wider *impact* of the behavior, and the need to *shift* that behavior - may be sufficient in terms of influence. If, however, at this point in the process there is still no clear sense of buy-in from the other party, then be prepared to discuss the potential *consequences* of the failure to demonstrate the required shift. What will happen if they don't comply? In what time frame? With what warnings? This is the stick rather than the carrot in terms of getting the donkey to move forward. If the person with the undesirable behavior is unable to shift simply by being made aware of the untenable situation and it's impacts on other people or other factors, then it may be necessary to use the extrinsic motivation of potential negative consequences in the event of failure to deliver.

Once again, it is most profitable to have the recipient do a lot of the talking, even in this 'potential consequences' stage. Remember, the key to getting people talking is asking them questions. I have had people in these kinds of conversations still resistant after working through the first three stages, so I'll ask them; "What do you think will happen if the desired shift doesn't happen?" Often, they answer, "I guess we'll have another chat then." I don't want to simply have another chat - and another one after that with no change - so I ask them to have another think about what the consequences might be if they fail to shift, because we're having *the chat* now! At this point they may jump straight to the conclusion of, "I might get sacked!" That's come from their own mouth, and though in most cases it is a little extreme, it is important for the unwilling recipient to think about the 'what if's' in the event of things not changing.

'Getoutoftheprincipalsofficeitis'

As I mentioned earlier, my headmaster had little influence on my behavior as a result of our 'chats' (the cane was somewhat more persuasive). When I talk about this story with my leadership course participants I ask them if they think that when the principal would finally ask me, "So do you understand?" do they think my response to him was, "I thought you started out well. I think that your emotions probably got the better of you somewhat in the middle, and then quite frankly I think you could have done a better job in summarizing what you'd talked about because you did lose me towards the end"? They obviously think that was the last thing I would say! Everyone unanimously agrees that my response would have been a simple, "yes" - not because I had understood, or even cared to understand, but because I was suffering from the disease of "Getoutoftheprincipalsofficeitis "!

A simple response seemed to work – no doubt because the principal was just as keen to see the back of me as I was of him. But each time he let me leave his office without making me really think about my inappropriate behavior, or process it's impacts, or understand the desired shift in me that he required, he missed an opportunity to influence my behavior. It would not have been too difficult to read my body language and see that I was not 'on board'. Had he made me think about the potential consequences of my actions he might have caused me to wake up to the hazardous track I was on.

The BISCuit model aims to give influencers a road map for structuring challenging conversations. This is vital because so often in these circumstances the recipients of these conversations have developed life-long strategies for deflecting and derailing them. As the old military adage goes "To be forewarned is to be forearmed." The better prepared we are for these conversations, the greater the likelihood of success for all parties concerned. So be prepared to: clarify behavior, elaborate on the impact of behavior, outline the shift required, and determine the potential consequences if the desired shift doesn't happen. The aim is to make shift happen!

CHAPTER SIX

WARM, CALM, HARD

"Whenever you're in conflict with someone there is one factor that can make the difference between damaging your relationship and deepening it. That factor is attitude."
William James

INTRODUCTION

There are moments for all of us in life where we encounter a customer who is unhappy with our service or product, or a staff member who is unhappy with a decision we have made. In these situations it pays to be fore-armed with insight regarding how to respond in a manner that will keep the door open for influence with that person - at least to the extent that we are able.

The 'Warm Heart, Calm Head, Hard Nose' Model is a model that I developed some years ago to help sales people dealing with unhappy, aggressive customers. I have since come to realize that this model is equally as useful in numerous other situations. It is a simple, three-step format for dealing with situations where escalating behavior requires an escalating response.

6.1

WARM HEART

This first response to unhappy customers, staff, or people in general should be a 'soft start up'. Remember, harsh criticism is not a helpful way to head towards a win-win in a conversation. We need to begin this process of dealing with an unhappy person with a 'Warm Heart'.

In the first instance, in any troublesome situation, we need to understand why the person is behaving the way they are. If someone is acting irritated or frustrated, we can seek to understand what is causing them to be frustrated. By discussing with them the reason for their irritation we create a mutual understanding between both parties as to what the problem really is, and why it is a problem. ***Sometimes, all that an irritated party needs is to feel heard and understood.*** In fact, the great majority of problems can be resolved simply by listening. Genuine listening keep's everyone's heart open to influence.

Part of this 'listening to understand' phase may involve asking questions to clarify how the problem has brought the person to this place of irritation. Make sure you really focus on listening to the answers to the questions you ask. Sometimes in the heat of battle our focus narrows to how we can get out of the situation and it becomes difficult to hear what the other person is saying, especially if we are

98

busy formulating a defense to their answer in our heads. It's necessary to remain focused on what they are saying and why they are saying it, which is critically important to the success of your efforts at this phase.

Maintaining a 'Warm Heart' will make it easier for you to reflect, clarify, and summarize the person's thoughts and feelings, which will in turn help them feel listened to. We need to ensure that we don't tell people that they are wrong to feel the way they are feeling. In this sense, we must be vigilant that we don't use the word '**but**': for example, "I understand how you're feeling, but you are quite incorrect in your assumption that…". The word 'but' is interpreted by the aggrieved party as; "Whatever I just said before the word 'but' I didn't actually mean…" 'But' can be a very dismissing word to use when responding to a complaint. Keep a check on your 'buts' as they can indicate a 'Below the Line' attitude.

Try and keep a warm heart even if the complaint has tipped over the line into a criticism. Don't react to any negative emotion accompanying their complaint, but rather try and be empathetic towards their situation. Assume the best and stay open to hearing what they need. If they are able to influence you at this phase, they are more likely to take your influence in the next phase.

Often in retail and service industries the first point of contact for a disgruntled customer is a staff member who actually has no ability or authority to rectify the problem, and who may have had nothing to do with the problem in the first place. Nonetheless the expectation from a customer or client is generally that we *care* that they have been inconvenienced or let down. To this end, a genuine apology can go a long way to easing the unhappiness. We may not be able to accept responsibility for what has happened, or failed to happen, but we can always apologize for how the customer is feeling as a result.

Sometimes all the customer really needs to know is that you do care about the plight they are in. Failing to offer an empathetic response (complete with accompanying body language and tone) may cause their negative demeanor to intensify because we failed to meet their number one expectation - that we care.

Through this process of resolving a problem with a disgruntled customer, it helps to be very aware of how you are feeling on the inside. There are two scenarios when being accused or held to account for something that's gone wrong: either it is your fault (or your company's fault), or it's not. If the latter is the case and you are being accused incorrectly, there's still room to apply the 'Warm Heart' approach and be genuinely sorry that the customer has not had their expectations met, or has been personally inconvenienced because of the situation.

The risk is that if you are feeling defensive because of their complaint your apology may come across as irritated or disingenuous, no matter how much you try to hide it. You need to set aside your feelings of defensiveness, which will only make matters escalate, and try your best not to become negatively emotionally involved in the complaint.

CALM HEAD

Our goal is to de-escalate the other person's negative state by keeping open to their needs emotionally and mentally. If, however, they are not willing to respond in kind, you may need to lay out the facts of the matter for them. Before we get to this point though, we need to make sure we have genuinely tried a 'Warm Heart' empathetic response, and kept our own responses free from defensiveness and contempt.

If this initial 'Warm Heart' approach fails to de-escalate the situation then approaching the person with a 'Calm Head' is the next responsive level. Use your mind to understand what the problem really is from their perspective. Take all the information they have given you, and the answers to the questions you have asked them (What? How? When? Where? Why?), and feedback to them your understanding of what the problem is and what they need from you, or what you need from them, to resolve it.

Focus on what you *can* do for them, without focusing on what *can't* be done. Rather than focusing on the negatives, focus on what *is* possible. It is helpful at this point to see the person and the problem as separate, having a sense that you and the customer are dealing with the problem 'shoulder to shoulder' rather than 'head to head'. You're

SOMETIMES ALL THAT AN IRRITATED PARTY NEEDS IS TO FEEL HEARD AND UNDERSTOOD.

on the same team trying to solve a common problem rather than adversaries competing against each other or fighting to win.

The customer may expect to have a battle with you to have their needs met, but *you* won't be having this battle with them and you may need to articulate this so they understand that there is no confrontation to be had, just a problem to be solved. Certainly, an antagonistic approach won't help matters. If the customer becomes aggressive you may need to make it clear that this kind of approach won't achieve their end goal of having the problem solved. It helps to move slowly and steadily, and for your sake as well as theirs, try to keep physical movements calm. If necessary repeat the facts without escalating the tone – try and keep your voice calm and level.

Using the 'Calm Head' approach may require us to sound like a 'broken record', repeating the message again and again whilst keeping calm. Of course, in all this you are trying your best to offer excellent customer service and take responsibility to resolve what you can.

6.3

HARD NOSE

At conferences and workshops where I have delivered this model, my 'Hard Nose' image is of a thick-skinned rhinoceros with its huge horn. It does require a thick skin to manage these kinds of aggravated interactions, and no more so than in the 'Hard Nose' phase. By this stage, you are almost in survival mode. The aggrieved party has not responded to genuine empathy and remorse, nor have they responded to authentic attempts to offer a remedy to the situation.

Nothing has worked to de-escalate their frustration and they have become irate, and so the final stage of being 'Hard Nosed' is all that remains. It is important to remind ourselves, even at this stage, that we must still try and view the person as separate from their behavior. Be prepared to speak to them with authority, whilst maintaining respect, being very clear with your boundaries in terms of not accepting aggressive behavior.

Flying Above the Line

I witnessed a superb example of this walking through a domestic airport one day. A passenger was extremely agitated and had begun to swear loudly at a staff member. As I walked past this scene on the way to my flight I overheard the staff member say, in a very authoritative and 'this is your final chance' tone, "Language like that won't help solve this… you need to stop speaking to me using that language if I'm going to sort this out for you." They were very clear and steadfast in their manner and even though I was in a hurry to catch my flight, in that short time I could hear the customer settle down to a more respectful and reasonable approach.

In attempting to influence an agitated person's behavior or attitude sometimes exposing them to elements of the impact of their poor behavior is necessary to help them realize that their behavior is having a detrimental effect on their own predicament, and also upon others, and is totally unacceptable.

If you are dealing with an irate customer, make clear that you need their behavior to calm down if you are to work with them to resolve their problem – and then clarify exactly what is going to be done

done to help resolve the issue. If an irate customer won't deescalate their frustration despite your attempts to listen and understand their problem, and if their behavior becomes increasingly frightening or even violent, inform them of the impact that behavior is going to have, which may even include calling in a higher authority (a manager, security, or even police) if necessary. Certainly, one broader impact of inappropriate or belligerent behavior from a customer is a stalling of the resolution of their issue.

It is very helpful to be clear on your 'Hard Nose' options in advance of these kinds of interactions so that you know what your personal tolerance threshold is for unacceptable behavior. At what point would you determine to walk away? When would you escalate to a manager? And what do you do when your manager is absent? It is even worth practicing your planned responses with someone you know or with another staff member. ***Train yourself by practicing*** asking them to calm down. Practice telling them what behavior you need them to change and the consequences if they don't. In the airport situation – the behavior was swearing, the impact was not having the problem solved, the shift was to stop swearing, and the consequences weren't required, but they may have ultimately been a refusal of services and a request to leave the premises (voluntarily or with assistance).

DEBRIEFING FROM A DIFFICULT INTERACTION

When dealing with difficult customers using the 'Warm Heart, Calm Head, Hard Nose' model empathy is your opening strategy. Alongside this, respect is key. Maintaining respect for the other party whilst maintaining respect for yourself also. Be aware of your attitude throughout these encounters because it is more than likely it will seep out via your body language and your tone. If you let yourself feel condescending or disinterested in the other person they are likely to pick up on that and things will get worse before they get better.

After these kinds of encounters, make sure you debrief with someone. Discuss with them; "What worked and why, and what seemed to escalate the situation?" ***You can learn a lot simply from reflecting on your own behavior*** and how that affected the customer's behavior, and visa versa. It is also helpful, in terms of your own learning and upskilling, to keep an eye out for examples of these situations being dealt with masterfully as you go through your day to day life. Learning from others is an easy and cost free way to gain insights into how best to cope with these situations.

If you work in customer service you may have dealt with the same problem a thousand times previously, but for the customer it may be their very first time, so it requires a concerted effort to avoid becoming 'battle weary', or worse still, 'battle hardened'. Keep in mind the support that you have from your management, and if nothing else works, remember that you are backed up by the laws of the land in terms of abuse on 'private property' and threats of violence. Regardless of what is said (or shouted, or thrown) at you remind yourself that you are a great person. Other people's 'junk' is their junk and not yours. Though you may be shaken up by aggressive or disgruntled people, don't let it impact your self-esteem! In the immortal words of pop singer Taylor Swift - "Shake it off!"

CHAPTER SEVEN

ROADMAPS TO WIN-WIN

"Win-win is a belief in the Third Alternative.
It's not your way or my way;
it's a better way, a higher way."
Stephen Covey

INTRODUCTION

I am frequently asked in training situations how to influence people who don't want to be influenced. Often this question is asked by course participants in leadership roles who want to know how to influence team members who are 'digging their toes in' on certain issues. This tends to be one of the easier scenarios in terms of influencing others, because at the end of the day the team leader or manager will have positional authority that they can lean on if they are unable to influence the team member without it.

How to influence others without that positional authority - be it a colleague, a neighbour, a customer or client, or ultimately even an up-line manager - is a much more challenging question. In these circumstances the concept of a 'win/win' approach is needed.

CHANGE THE RADIO FM STATION!

A win/win occurs when you carefully consider in advance, **'WiiFT'** (What's in it For Them?) - when you are thoughtful towards the other person's needs and feelings and desired outcomes. When you think of others who will also be affected by your decisions and actions, you will make the process of influencing others more effective than simply handling the situation without thinking past **'WiiFM'** (What's in it For Me?) Certainly, I have seen many people over the years attempt to influence others with a 'Win/I don't care about your needs' point of view, which does little to endear the other party to considering a shift to our desired position. If this is where your tuning is set you need to change your radio station to WiiFM!

Four Wrongs Don't Make a Right

Many years ago, I worked for a manager who I got on well with, but at times our different cultural backgrounds meant we didn't always see eye to eye on how I managed my team. On one occasion, she sent me an email informing me that I had made four serious errors of judgement in my role. That would have been okay, and we could have negotiated our way through the various issues normally, but she chose for some unfortunate reason to copy our entire Board of Governors into the email. As you can imagine, I was quite distressed by this, not so much for the fact of how it might reflect on me - in fact quite the opposite. Three of the four assertions or accusations were quite unfounded and the fourth was not entirely true either, and easily explained. Either way this meant that it was more her reputation than mine that was likely to suffer, firstly for copying in the Board on what were work related issues that were her responsibility to deal with, and secondly because she was now going to have to face the Board once the facts of the matter had been disclosed to her. She would need to dig herself out of the hole that she had created.

It would have been very easy for me to have stepped away from her and let the 'lightning strike as it may'. I could have easily become offended by her accusations and felt justified in letting her suffer the consequences of her thinking and rash action, but I wanted to have an ongoing working relationship with her once she came away from explaining the erroneous email to the Board and I genuinely wanted her not to be hurt by this mistake. So, having considered the issue overnight, I approached her to help her to clean up the mess that she had made. I did this by booking a meeting with her, and once I had explained the facts of the matter I then went on to say that "we" had some work to do to clear the issue up as far as the Board was concerned. My manager could see in my attitude and in my demeanor that I was wanting this to work out as well as it possibly could for her as well as myself, and she gratefully worked with me to formulate a plan to rectify the issue with the Board.

If I had just stood back and watched her struggle in explaining her actions to the Board, I may have achieved a 'win' for myself, but it would have been a 'lose' for her. 'Win/lose' is never the best kind of 'win' to achieve. Even in sports, constant winning becomes tedious and uninspiring.

Winning Ain't Everything!

My favorite sports team in the world are the "All Blacks", our national rugby team. They are (the only) three-times World Rugby Champions, they are the most successful rugby team in the history of the game. Many people suggest that they are the most successful international team in any sport ever.

I love it when the All Blacks win! They set a new world record in 2016 clocking up 18 consecutive international wins! But I was not the only person who found the constant and convincing wins somewhat mundane to watch. There is nothing better than a closely fought win where the All Blacks manage to triumph in the dying stages of the game. In this sense, it feels like a 'win/win' for the game in general - with my team just fractionally winning a little more than the opposition! Runaway wins game after game are not great for the game of rugby or for the All Blacks and their form. It was interesting that after their world record 18-win streak they lost to Ireland for the first time in their 111-year history of playing each other!

If we constantly look to win at the expense of others it will eventually come back to bite us. Winning in that sense is only a short-term success because our ability to influence others will diminish if their experience with us is one of constantly coming off second best. It was in my best interests and my manager's best interests, in the earlier story, that I approached the situation with a 'win/win' frame of mind. It was this approach that ultimately gave the best possible short and long term outcome.

On a side note - if you do receive contentious information via email or text or social media, make sure you don't respond by simply hitting 'reply'. Instead go face to face and hear the person's issues where you can also watch their body language and have instant access to their answers. Sometimes 'old fashioned' just works!

What We Need is a Hole!

Some years ago, I was contracted to deliver two-hour long seminars to members of the public on the subject of website design and development. As part of the content I needed to emphasize that research had discovered that a website would generate better results if the headline, and in particular the home page headline, focused on the benefits of the business' product or service.

As a way of illustrating this concept I talked about a website selling drill bits. I would begin the illustration by asking the audience; "Hands up those of you who have ever needed a drill bit?" Naturally a number of people would raise their hands. Then I would inform them, tongue in cheek, that it was my understanding that no one has ever needed a drill bit! What people are actually in need of is *holes*! As an example, I used a hypothetical story of Bob, the owner of the ABC Plumbing Company, who also had a subsidiary drill bit sales business. Having heard the importance of a good home page headline, Bob had turned up to the web design office having drafted a headline that said; "New and improved auger bit with a 'next-generation' tungsten carbide cutting edge and unique screw-tip technology." In trying to focus the home page headline on the attributes of his new auger bit, Bob would no doubt end up missing the real needs of the customer he was trying to reach – which was what they could *do* with the drill bit. In actual fact what customers were really looking for are smooth and flawless holes - so they need auger bits that don't burn softwoods and don't splinter upon exiting the timber. Bob's communication needed to respond to the real need of the customer - it needed to translate the benefits to the customer rather than leaving it to the customer to make that translation themselves from features to benefits.

This is the challenge that we have in attempting to influence or 'sell' someone an idea that they may not naturally want to 'buy' into. We need to move beyond communicating the nature of the change, or even the way in which the change would benefit others or the business, and think about the ways in which it is likely to benefit the person we are actually trying to influence. This may mean that we should do more homework prior to approaching the party that we're hoping to influence to determine what a 'win' might look like in terms of what they want, or need, or hope for.

Dealing with a Hire Power

In the late 1980's and early 90's I was training unemployed young people and preparing them for work in fields including the 'sports, fitness and leisure industry'. As part of this training it was necessary to prepare them for interviews for either tertiary training or for relevant sector employment. One of the shifts that was required in my students' thinking was to put themselves in the shoes of their prospective tutors or future employers. As part of this process I would draw an image of a radio on the whiteboard - complete with dials, a speaker, and a sparking antenna. I would then tell the learners that employers are only able to tune in to one radio station and that is WiiFM which stands for, "What's In It For Me?!?" It was necessary for my students to change from thinking that employers were simply waiting to give them a job – to realizing that the employers were looking to have a need met, and they were looking for employees who could meet that need. The former thinking would cause applicants to present themselves as 'job beggars' rather than as potential assets for the hiring organization. Instead I helped my trainees to understand the needs of the business or educational institution they were applying to, and what the bigger purpose was behind the interview questions they would be asked. So rather than walking into an interview focusing on what was in it for them (WiiFm) as an applicant in terms of work conditions and remuneration, they were much better prepared to interview well because they had considered in advance; "What's in it for the employer?" This gave them an entirely different perspective during the interview.

The more we consider what is in it for them, rather than simply "what's in it for me?", the greater the likelihood we will be able to influence people toward a positive outcome by understanding and appealing to the benefits of the suggested change from their perspective. In my previous story of my former manager who had emailed her Board inappropriately, it would have been the easiest thing in the world for me to 'hang her out to dry', so to speak. I could have done that by offering her no support or assistance whatsoever, but that would have been a very poor choice on my part. It may have achieved a short-term gain in terms of vindication, but potentially a long-term pain given that I wanted to continue to work with this manager in the future. I realized that if she fared poorly, then that would have some kind of flow on effect to me, even though that was not my primary motive for wanting to help her out of the sticky situation she had gotten herself into. The philosophy that I approached her with was a 'win-win.' I was happy to have her 'win' in the situation but I was aware that her win would also be my win in the long run. As a result of the approach that day she was very grateful and we went on to have a positive working relationship when that could have easily been the beginning of a real downhill slide. I would have been justified to think that the decision she made was hers to rectify and she was responsible for mending the relationship 'tear' she had caused, but instead it was my attitude and response that determined whether our relationship would deteriorate or be redeemed.

7.2

THE DOOR OF INFLUENCE

Communication is fundamental to being human. Given that communication is such a universally practiced activity, I find it fascinating that very few people are clear on what they see as being the ultimate goal of their communication. When I ask people on my training programs to define the goal I receive very disparate replies. Few people have a clearly defined goal in mind when communicating with others. Sure, we all have unspoken goals and subconscious intentions, but we seldom take the time to reflect on what these are. None of us just communicate to be heard, we communicate to have what we say received by the hearer. We communicate to influence and be influenced.

Nothing to Shout About

I find myself these days predominantly involved in the training of leaders, and as a result the subject of how to influence management above you comes up again and again. Influencing management 'further up the food chain', or *'leading up', takes as much skill and emotional intelligence as it does to lead those in your care.* As part of the logic of effectively influencing those in authority over you, it's important to understand the goal of communication, and how to achieve it.

In my training when I ask people to come up with a commonly understood definition of the goal of communication I get replies such as; "The transfer of information", or, "Two parties having common understanding". I'll write these definitions down on a piece of flipchart nod vigorously. People reluctantly agree that I achieved their communication goal definitions, but more than one person in the room will tell me that although I achieved the goal, I did it poorly by risking irreparable damage to the relationship.

I then draw two doors on a flipchart; one door is closed with several locks holding it shut, and another door is slightly ajar. Above those two doors I write in large letters, 'The Door of Influence', and I explain that the ultimate goal of communication is not merely the transfer of information, rather the ultimate goal is that who-ever I am communi-cating with is *even more open to my influence* in the future, as a result of our present encounter.

If I want people to not only hear me, but to be influenced by what I say both in the short and the long term, I need to be aware of the 'Relational Bank Account' that I am either 'depositing' into or 'withdrawing' from through my communication and interaction. At the very core of this communication event is the notion of *trust*. Is the way that I am communicating to this person building trust or causing it to erode? Communication that builds trust deposits into the 'Relational Bank Account'. Communication that erodes trust withdraws from the emotional bank account.

Trust is crucial when communicating up-line to management. 'What' you are communicating is nowhere near as important as 'how' you communicate in terms of opening the 'Door of Influence'. Most of the people that I train have genuine and bona fide issues to address with management, but the way that they communicate those issues ultimately determines how much influence the speaker is likely to gen-erate with the listener. If I communicate with someone in such a way that they have understood my message, but the level of influence that I have with them diminishes, then I have not achieved the ultimate goal of communication.

Remember the earlier story where I met a young man at the gym with a large swastika tattooed onto his head? I would have liked to have challenged the ideology of that young man and maybe some-day we will have that conversation, but I know he would only be open to that conversation if my earlier interactions with him had motivated him to 'open the door' to my influence rather than shut that door and lock it permanently! I was able to ask him some quite personal questions and get some honest answers only because I had opened the 'Door of Influence' by showing a genuine interest in his story. I had built a level of trust with him and consequently made emotional deposits into our 'Relational Bank Account'.

It is not prudent to communicate with people and have them comply with our requests in the short term if how we do it means we lose our ability to influence them in the long term. Of course, communication *is* about getting our ideas across in a manner that people understand, but if the manner in which we communicate causes ill-will to increase, and trust to diminish, then regardless of the immediate effect we could not consider that to be effective communication in the bigger scheme of things.

Successful influencers are those who are clear in their communication, and who **check that understanding has occurred** as a result of their communication. They are conscious of the more important goal of maintaining or even improving the relationship through the manner of their interaction. They think long term. They are cognizant of the fact that gaining influence with others is not a quick fix. It is a long term process that comes from building trust with people through consistent positive deposits into the 'Relational Bank Account' that we have with them. It's not just what we say – it's how we say it that matters!

CHAPTER EIGHT

BUILDING BETTER BELIEFS

"Often the difference between someone who can't and someone who can is our belief in them."
Glen Sharkey

INTRODUCTION

Martin Luther King Junior lived at a time in the history of the United States when many people who had an inherent disdain for racism, both Caucasian and African-American, would have had no hope of seeing an integrated America in their lifetime. King was different. He lived and breathed his belief in change and is recorded as having said; "I refuse to accept the view that mankind is so tragically bound to the starless midnight of racism and war that the bright daybreak of peace and brotherhood can never become a reality... I believe that unarmed truth and unconditional love will have the final word." He was proved correct as his sacrificial efforts and his unwavering belief brought about a rapid shift to the racist cultural structure in the US. As leaders in any arena, having a strong belief that other people can grow, shift, and better themselves, whether it be in their role as spouses, parents, staff members or managers, is fundamental to our ability to influence them towards change.

I work with a broad spectrum of participants in my training, from people at the front lines of the workforce through to senior leaders, from people who absolutely love the opportunity for personal and professional development through to what we in the facilitation industry call 'hostages' (people who have been sent to training against their will and better judgement). One of the reasons that I achieve transformational change with so many people is that I have an inherent belief that *everyone* can achieve better results.

If we are to be great leaders who can successfully influence others, we need to be equally as able to influence ourselves. At the conclusion of one eight-month leadership training program I informed the program participants that they didn't need to be in a formal facilitated program to achieve that outstanding personal change. I went on to say that at the end of every year I can look back at goals that I have had for my personal development and I am able to cite specific examples of becoming a better professional trainer and speaker, and a better individual in my personal relationships, as each year passes. My foundational belief that everyone is capable of positive change is solidly anchored in my own experience of bettering myself over the years. I'm by no means perfect, in fact because of just how imperfect I am, there is so much room in so many areas for me to make improvement. But one thing I have focused on is self-improvement through self-leadership.

8.1

BUILDING A HIGH BAR

Think about three different types of leaders that you have known: a leader at work; a personal leader such as a grandparent, a coach, or a youth group leader; and then also a leader that you may admire from a distance such as a political leader from history. *If you were to list as many of the positive attributes of those leaders as you can what would your list consist of?*

I often do this exercise as part of leadership courses. The flip-chart that I write participants' responses up onto is generally the most photographed piece of paper during the entire training. There is something very personal, very captivating, and very powerful about such a list of key traits of people whose leadership has been respected and admired. This list is both inspiring and somewhat intimidating - it sets the bar very high. A list like this can be very helpful to reflect on as you set your own goals for your leadership aspirations.

I have a strong belief that I can do better. I often share my personal vision for this with my course attendees. That then becomes a platform for me influencing them in their own journeys to become better leaders. If I didn't believe that people are capable of higher achievement, not only in terms of work performance, but also as it pertains to relational success, character development, and physical well-being, I wouldn't have the authority to encourage them towards that kind of improvement. ***The sincerity of my belief in others being able to improve is imperative to my influencing them towards personal growth.***

All Things Are Possible

I often encourage my participants to set a health and wellness goal to be completed over a three-month period. Health and wellness goals are highly motivating for short term periods because people can almost always tangibly see and feel the improvements they are aiming for in this time. I don't think I'd be able to influence attendees to look so seriously at their physical wellness if I didn't believe that everyone in the room was capable of achieving more in this area.

I also regularly show a video of the father and son duo called 'Team Hoyt'. The son has cerebral palsy, and the father, who was not previously a runner, decided to make his son's dream come true by taking him on a five mile charity run. He managed this by laboriously pushing him in a buggy. This activity gave them both joy and a great sense of accomplishment. Over time the father and son progressed on to larger and larger runs until they eventually began competing together in marathons and finally in 'Ironman' events, where the father tows the son in an inflatable boat for the five-mile swim, peddles the hundred-mile bike ride with his son on a seat on the front of the bike, and then finally pushes him in a buggy for the marathon run. The video that we watch is titled 'Father of the Century' but I preface the video by stating that, although it focuses on fatherhood, it is inspiring from a leadership perspective also. I use this video as an encouragement that each one of us can always do more than we might think we can. I wouldn't or couldn't say that if I didn't truly believe that we are all capable of greater things than we are currently doing.

THE ONE WITH THE MOST HOPE
BUILDS THE MOST INFLUENCE

If we want to be an effective leader we need to choose our words carefully and deliberately. We need to become intentional in our communication. The same is true for anyone in any role who wants to increase their influence with others. But ***what we say is nowhere near as important as how we say it***. We communicate feeling, passion, and ultimately influence, primarily through our congruent body language, tone and the words we chose to use. If our body language, tone of voice, and words don't line up and have an intrinsic congruence, our influence will be compromised.

Both hope and hopelessness, despite being intangibles, can be felt very strongly. If a team leader succumbs to hopelessness in a trying situation this will be communicated through their language as well as their general demeanor. Demeanor is catchy! If we have a negative disposition as leaders, expect it to become contagious!

Our hope or hopelessness in situations can become a self-fulfilling prophecy. If I believe I can influence a person I will have a much better chance of doing so – of aligning my actions with my thoughts. If I believe that I can't influence a person then it is highly likely I will make no effort to do so. Henry Ford summed this up when he said, "If you think you can do a thing, or think you can't do a thing, you're probably right!" I'm also much more likely to have a positive impact on others if I come from a hopeful and therefore positive outlook, rather than a fatalistic or even pessimistic viewpoint. Napoleon Bonaparte is quoted as having said; ***"Leaders are dealers in hope."*** Military leaders may have more opportunity and greater necessity than workplace leaders in maintaining hope for the sake of the troops in the face of life threatening circumstances, but leaders in the workplace are just as responsible for maintaining levels of hope in order to get the job done as effectively and efficiently as possible. Workers in everyday workplaces all face trying and difficult situations at times. Keeping up hope in the face of difficult circumstances is an important trait of effective leaders.

8.3

WORDS BUILD WORLDS

Aligning our beliefs with our body language and words is a necessity if we want to become a great influencer. It is also ethical. If we don't fundamentally believe something is possible, we shouldn't be expecting others to believe it. Body language is a huge component of communication, but the power of words can't be under-estimated either. ***The words we choose to use can open the door of influence when working with others, or can shut it up tight.*** People who are effective influencers of others are very intentional with the language they choose. They aim where possible to be uplifting, hopeful, motivating and encouraging, even if they're attempting to influence significant and costly change to the one being influenced. Words build worlds. The more intentional and careful I am in my choice of language the more likely I am to have a positive influence with those around me, and as the old saying goes, "Choose your words carefully - because you may end up having to eat them!"

Need You Say More??

Toastmasters is an international public speaking club and as part of the process for developing speakers they have a feedback system called CRC which stands for 'Commend, Recommend, Commend'. Recently I was given cause to reflect on this feedback system when I was discussing it with my leadership course participants. One of my participants, on hearing about 'CRC', reacted scornfully and described it as "a B@## S&%# sandwich!"

After his exclamation, he refused to expand on his thinking around this. I took time overnight to consider his response and the next day I addressed it. I said to the group that it was not his perspective regarding CRC that was so much a learning point for us as a group, but rather the manner in which he had articulated his difference of opinion. I went on to say that there is a way that we communicate with others that opens them up to our perspective, and ultimately to our influence, and there is a way we communicate that closes people off and shuts them down. I suggested that the way that he had communicated yesterday was much more the latter than the former. It came across in a contemptuous fashion and did nothing to open the group up to his thinking or warm us up to shifting our perspective. Whenever we exhibit contempt for others' thoughts, feelings, or actions, we shut and lock the door to influence in their lives. ***Contempt is toxic to relationships.*** This is one of the reasons CRC is effective – because it makes us think about the good and the valuable in a person and their behavior, and not just what we want them to change. This has the effect of reducing any contempt that we may have towards them.

This turned out to be an excellent learning opportunity for this participant and for the whole class. The way he had communicated actually caused people to think less of his opinion - rather than as highly as he might have actually deserved (being a very intelligent guy with some great ideas). He had communicated to us in 'turtle' fashion – popping out of his shell to lob a hand grenade into the conversation, then quickly reverting into his shell and not being open to on-going dialogue on the issue. He didn't 'stay out' long enough to engage in meaningful conversation that might have helped us to understand why he disagreed, and in what ways our thinking could improve as a result of taking influence from his thinking.

Often people who communicate this way are trying to protect their ego. They may feel too vulnerable to expose themselves personally to other people's opinions of them. Consequently they limit people's ability to question their line of thought. The irony is that this kind of communication actually makes people think less of you rather than more. In putting up a wall to protect ourselves from other people's negative opinions, we inadvertently become a creator of those opinions!

Rewording is Rewarding

My leadership training participants are often required to present projects at the end of the course. I had a participant some time ago stand-up and present on his project. During his practice presentation, he lobbed out this comment; "We have not been able to proceed with this project at this point because people are just too lazy!" He was one of the younger leaders on the course, with a lot of potential but not a lot of leadership experience. One of his challenges had already been identified as becoming increasingly professional in the work environment, so that over time he would be able to gain the respect that he needed to effectively lead others.

At the end of the practice I commended him for how well he had done and then highlighted the language that he had used. I explained to him that using the word 'lazy' to describe people in general was a derogatory and accusatory term. I challenged him and the rest of the participants to think of alternative ways to convey the same message but with more hopeful, professional language.

He and other participants made suggestions like; "The team is not yet at the point of understanding the importance of this process", and, "Various team members are yet to pick up this practice as business-as-usual." These were much more professional ways of saying the same thing, but would present the participant in a far better light than someone who was simply frustrated by the lack of engagement from his team. Additionally, if he altered this kind of wording externally, it would help him to alter his internal understanding of his team. Seeing his team in a more positive light would then help him to reconsider his strategies for getting the team on board. If they were just lazy – there truly was no hope. If they are 'yet to understand' then there is still hope and new options become possible for moving the project along, particularly in regards to him taking ownership for assisting their understanding.

Being a leader, and being someone who can influence others, requires us to see further ahead than others might, and see potential where others can't. We are the bringers of hope, the ones who can see a way forward into the future and who can express this way forward so others will join us on the journey into that future.

CHAPTER NINE

COURAGE

INTRODUCTION

Influencers see a better future and help others move forward into that future. This requires courage. The notion of courage and its relationship to influence is a fascinating one. The antithesis of courage is fear. As much as we need to understand what courage is in our attempts to influence others positively, we also need to examine fear and its manifest forms. These forms might include stress, tension, anxiety, and even timidity.

Courage doesn't replace fear - it is just required in amounts that are ***in excess of*** the fear that is present in order to provide the impetus to move forward. I don't have to overcome all my fears to have that tough conversation with a child, a workmate, or a boss. I just need enough courage to cause me to broach that difficult conversation - despite present fears. A brave person is seldom a fearless person!

SWIMMING AGAINST THE TIDE

When it comes to influencing others, there are times and places where it may be necessary to go against the tide of popular opinion. This is seldom comfortable and never easy, as the metaphor of swimming against the tide implies.

When I am presenting training I often encounter participants who don't look after themselves in terms of health and well-being. Their diets appear to be poor and their physical exercise hovers somewhere between very little and none. I am swimming against the tide of the general populace in the room by encouraging people towards healthier lifestyles and improved fitness but I am more than prepared to do this knowing it will benefit not only them, but also their families, and the companies they work for. Swimming against the tide is not the most comfortable practice but if it is necessary to positively influence people then not only should it be embarked upon as a course of action – it is the right thing to do.

BEING AN INFLUENCER REQUIRES COURAGE TO SWIM AGAINST THE TIDE OF POPULAR OPINION.

The Best Defense to a Bad Offence

Many years ago, I found myself in a crowded takeaway restaurant. I was in one of a number of queues, each with quite a few people in them, waiting to order my food. To one side of the queues I could hear, in fact the entire restaurant could hear, a customer severely berating a staff member over the price of a small hamburger. It seemed that everyone in the restaurant was feeling pretty uncomfortable by the scene and by how helpless the staff member seemed in the face of such unpleasant hostility.

Something rose inside me and I said in a voice that could be heard by the irate customer (and by necessity, everyone around me); "Why don't you just leave her alone?" The customer turned around and said something back to me in an attempt to justify his aggression and I replied something along the lines of; "Is this really worth it just for the cost of the hamburger?" Thankfully the customer abandoned their quest for justice and walked out of the store and as they did I looked up and I could see a young, large Pacific Island man working at the back near the grill with a big smile on his face. Clearly, he had appreciated someone standing up for his manager, no doubt something that he would have had very little trouble in doing so himself if company policy permitted it.

Generosity in Spades

Although it is a commendable trait to stick up for people who are being treated poorly, ***there are ways to deal with hostile situations where everyone's dignity can remain intact*** and everyone can walk away from the situation feeling like they have had their needs met. I have no doubt that in the previous story there was a need to address an unfair attitude towards a salesperson and it was helpful for me to speak up and swim against the tide when no one else in the situation was prepared to say anything, regardless of how they felt. However, a better outcome is always going to be a win-win for both the unhappy customer and the sales-person.

Recently I was in a large building supplies store. I just had a few small things to purchase and so it was going to be a very quick trip, however I stepped into the checkout queue just in time to be slowed down by an irate customer ahead of me demanding that a spade be replaced due to a broken handle. The salesperson was attempting to explain to the customer that they were unable to replace the spade because of a store policy stating that replacement of faulty products could only occur with the customer producing the original purchase receipt. As the customer didn't have a purchase receipt, but clearly wanted the replacement, the situation became increasingly loud and unhappy.

As the situation continued to escalate I called out in a very helpful and non-confrontational tone; "How much is that replacement spade?" The customer replied in a very agitated tone; "It's only a few dollars but they're refusing to replace it because I can't prove that I've purchased it from here!" I then said; "Look, I'm just about to purchase my items - why don't you give me the replacement spade and I'll pay for it myself?" This was a solution that I was genuinely willing to offer to calm the situation down. It did exactly that. The customer completely de-escalated but said to me; "There's no need to do that, but thank you so much, that's a very generous offer. I'd just like to sort it out with the staff here but I really appreciate you offering to do that." He continued to negotiate with the salesperson in a much quieter and calmer tone. Having his need heard and a solution offered went a long way towards deescalating his angst.

Rather than telling the irate customer to leave the salesperson alone, as I did many years ago in the fast food store, I've now developed other ways of influencing people's behavior while *leaving everyone's dignity as intact as possible*. When I make the effort to consider the perspective and needs of both parties in these circumstances I then maximize my chances of positively influencing all parties, rather than just myself and the poor salesperson.

Not every situation can be a win-win, but courage can be shown in more ways than simply standing up to poor behavior. The thing about courage though is that it works best with an element of personal generosity – personal sacrifice – no matter how that is delivered.

More Than Just Warming the Bench

Many years ago I started playing for a new football team in a small New Zealand town. It has always surprised me that players will turn up to football training with all the waterproof gear they need on a cold and wet winter's evening but when it comes to game day there seems to be some unwritten rule that you are not to wear anything else but the team jersey and possibly one undergarment. That doesn't suit me. I will wear up to three thermal undergarments during the first half on wet and freezing winter days, and at half time I take them off and change into fresh dry thermals. I also wear a beanie, and sometimes even two! As a professional speaker, I don't have the luxury of being able to take sick leave on a Monday morning because I caught a cold as a result of spending an hour and a half in awful weather on Saturday afternoon. Therefore, it is in my interests to stay dry, or to at least stay warm.

I've been laughed at for years by other football players because of the amount of clothing I wear to stay warm during wintery games, so when I turned up to play for my new team I expected to receive the same treatment. I put my beanie on when we were about to play in a very strong wind with an unusually cold chill factor. Many of the players commented on how cold the wind was, with some even making joking remarks about postponing the game.

When one of my fellow players saw that I had my beanie on he commented on it, thinking that I had inadvertently forgotten to take it off prior to stepping on the field. When I informed him that I intended to play with it on he asked me if I was some kind of 'poofter' (New Zealand slang for a weaker mortal!) I just smiled at him and carried on, not wishing to get into a negative interaction at the start of the game. No more was said about my choice of apparel for the game, and it was clear that my fellow player remained unimpressed by my departure from traditional football attire.

Fast forward to the end of year football tournament which was forecast for the worst weather that we had played in all year. During our third game of the tournament we experienced the heaviest rain of the day and I couldn't help but be amused when I looked across and both players next to me, like myself, had beanies on during the game. The thing that fascinated me the most was that the very guy who had called me a 'poofter' several weeks earlier was playing alongside me in - you guessed it - his own beanie! As you can imagine, I was tempted to make a comment or two, but as Dale Carnegie would say, "That would have been poor form"!

At the same tournament, we were together in the changing

rooms during the lunch break and our goalkeeper was complaining about having to put his wet goalie jersey back on. He was astounded to watch me change into dry thermals and absolutely flabbergasted when I took my boots and my socks off and put on dry socks for the afternoon matches. Of course, I then experienced the mockery and ridicule that I've come to expect in this set of circumstances where I am bucking the trend and going against the grain, but he was certainly green with 'dry-outfit envy' and I won't be at all surprised to see this goalkeeper taking a leaf out of my book and making more of an effort to keep himself warm in the future.

No doubt there is an idiom, or at least there should be, that it is better to be a dry and mocked team member than a wet and freezing one! The previous story is not a terribly noble or self-sacrificing anecdote of 'swimming against the tide' but it does serve to illustrate the point that to influence people's decisions or behaviors it may be necessary to behave somewhat counter-culturally, letting people know in the first instance that there is an alternative to the status quo, and in the second instance providing them with an example that going against the flow is both possible and beneficial. I certainly didn't set out to change the mindsets or the dress code of my fellow football players, but in being prepared to hold my ground against both convention and peer pressure it clearly had an influential outcome.

9.2

IN COURAGE

What my fellow footballers choose to wear to protect themselves against the elements, or not, is entirely their own decision. However, some of us find ourselves in positions of influence in the workplace, in families, or in community groups that do require us to swim against the tide, hold that position, and see others in our charge change their direction also. This requires a kind of courage that comes from a clear belief that beneficial change is possible, and that it will be well worth the cost.

The Need to In-Courage our Kids

Many years ago, my then seven-year-old daughter was playing in a Saturday morning football league. On the side-line, I could hear another father ten meters away from me ranting loudly at his son throughout the entire first half. There was nothing the boy could do that was right in the eyes of his father. Although the boy made mistakes and wasn't a perfect player, there was still ample room to encourage him, so I found my discomfort rising as he continued to discourage and disparage his son. His disparagement of his son's playing was so bad that I wanted to yell at the father to stop, but of course I knew that this would do nothing to improve the situation for the son. While pondering what to do the face of the founder of the family support organization "Parenting with Confidence" - Ian Grant - popped into my head, and I began to think to myself, "What would Ian Grant do?"

Finally, the whistle went for half time and I wandered up to this father (who was at least six inches taller than me) and said to him; "I've been listening to your comments towards your son during the first half and wondered if he might respond better if you were to encourage him more?" His eyes tightened and he looked down and me and said in a somewhat menacing tone; "Are you telling me I'm not very encouraging?" It looked like the encounter was going to disintegrate into a physical altercation.

Although I had felt concerned at listening to his comments towards his son I also knew that it was important not to come across as critical so I maintained a very calm tone and talked to him more about the positive ways he could try communicating with his son. I was both pleased (and relieved) when he then thanked me for my comments and said that he would try to focus on being more encouraging. The second half was a much more pleasurable experience and although I did not witness effervescent encouragement and support from the father to the son, there was a marked decline in his discouragement.

Many people might consider that it was none of my business to address this father on his manner with his son, and my detractors may well be right. However, I have appreciated well-intentioned and genuinely caring people challenging my own behavior over the years, and on the occasions that I haven't listened when I should have, the fault has generally lain with me. *I have benefited from the courage that people have displayed in addressing my flaws*, including learning the value of needing to have courage on occasions in attempting to influence others. Indeed, it was Ian Grant's own courage in speaking forthrightly to father's in New Zealand about showing kindness to their children that had influenced me to speak up on this occasion.

Rise to the Challenge

I had a participant on my leadership training recently who required quite a mindset shift in order to improve his leadership credibility. Many of his comments to others on the course were negative and unconstructive and he was inclined to interject foul language into these comments. After a day of this I addressed his attitude in front of the group and issued him a challenge. I told the participant and the group that I would only issue this kind of challenge a couple of times a year with the hundreds of people that I work with, and only to people that I believe are 'up for it'. I also only issue this kind of challenge to people who have genuine potential for leadership influence.

The challenge is something that I picked up from motivational expert Tony Robbins. It requires people to attempt ***seven-days of not speaking negatively on a single occasion***. I don't know exactly how Tony Robbins sets up the challenge but the way I issue it to participants is that they must do seven consecutive days without saying anything negative, critical or defensive. If for instance they make a negative comment at the beginning of the second day, then the clock starts again and the first day and a half doesn't count. The aim is to do seven consecutive days without speaking negatively.

One of the other participants on the course asked if the challenge required not thinking negative thoughts either and I answered that it is merely what we speak rather than what we think. It's hard enough to stop articulating negative thoughts – it is virtually impossible to stop thinking them, particularly immediately. So, what I was actually challenging the participant to do was to be aware of his negative thoughts and censor them before they made it out in speech. Of course, the ultimate purpose of this challenge is not simply to avoid speaking negatively but to be aware of the sheer quantity that some of us spend in negative talk and how incredibly pervasive negative thinking and speech can be.

I define negative speech as *any negative talk that has no intent nor possibility of achieving a constructive outcome*. For example, I don't enjoy or even respect some of the television reality dramas that other people in my family enjoy watching. Sometimes I find myself drawn in to watching a show over their shoulder, and I've been known to make derogatory remarks about the subjects or intent of the show. This would be a perfect example of negative talk. The subjects of the show, or the show's director, are unable to hear my comments and so the negative nature of the remark has no constructive intent or potential to change the show in any way. What I am ultimately doing is just taking the opportunity to reinforce my 'negative-muscle memory'.

When I go to the gym to do a physical workout I do a lot of pushing and pulling but I don't achieve any productive work. What I do manage to achieve is a strengthening of those muscles used in the various exercises. In the same way, when I'm negative about any people that aren't present, I am merely working out my negativity muscles and building their strength for subsequent situations. A lot of people have become very fit in the area of negativity through decades of work outs! They have spent so long in the 'Negativity gymnasium' that they have become muscle bound and inflexible!

On the other hand, it's okay for me to sit down with one of my team members and talk to them about their poor performance or bad attitude. That's not negative because my intent is to be constructive. This kind of conversation has every potential for having a profitable outcome, and certainly when I have these kinds of conversations, that is what I am hoping and aiming for.

In issuing a negativity challenge I am careful to choose people who I really think can accept such a challenge, and who will **benefit from peer accountability**. When I issue a challenge like this I frame it in such a way that it is almost seen as a privilege to be deemed worthy of such a challenge. There are generally people in the room who are more negative than the participant that I pick on but who are not capable of entertaining the idea of such a challenge because they are unaware of the extent of their negativity and are not ready to embrace such confronting news. I also refrain from challenging people who I doubt are in a place in their journey to see any benefit in such a challenge. Lastly, it's not worth challenging people publicly if there's any chance they might react poorly to having the issue of their negativity highlighted in a group setting.

While I must be very careful and discerning when I issue a challenge publicly, when I do there is something very powerful, and empowering that occurs. The bonus of highlighting the issue and giving a public challenge is that those who are not yet ready for such a challenge can quietly consider their own negativity and may even enter into the same process privately.

It is a risk to have to read the person and the situation accurately and conclude that the outcome will be a constructive one. Even once that judgment call has been made, it still takes courage to challenge individual participants amongst their peers, but I've learnt over the years that the **results of the challenge are more than worth it.** In taking the time to talk privately with the participant during the morning tea break I was pleased to hear him acknowledge the fact that he had been thinking recently that his nature was becoming somewhat negative and he willingly accepted the challenge.

If you want to be someone who truly has a positive influence on others it is going to require you to start exercising your courage muscles. As with all exercise - exercising courage becomes easier the more you do it. Courage is contagious - so if you want to know how effective your exercise is being - look at your team - or those around you - and see how courageous they are being with their own influence. You will no doubt be rubbing off on them!

CHAPTER TEN

COURAGEOUS CONVERSATIONS

*"It takes courage to grow up
and turn out to be who you really are."*
E. E. Cummings

INTRODUCTION

Being able to effectively conduct courageous conversations is a key element of leadership competence. It doesn't require courage to go to someone and say, "I'm really not sure how to tell you this, but there's just no other way to break it to you so I guess I should just be straight up - we going to give you a pay rise!" It doesn't require courage to deliver good news, it is the difficult and potentially contentious conversations that require a good deal of courage. These are the kind of conversations I label 'Courageous Conversations'. Every leader must have them at some stage in their career, and generally many times over.

PLANNING AHEAD

The vast majority of difficult work-based conversations are between mature people who are professional enough, and sufficiently focused, to discuss even contentious issues in a respectful manner. It's the conversations where one or other person lacks that maturity that are not easy to have. These are the conversations that people tend to shy away from, particularly those who are in the early stages of their leadership journey. The factor that often holds people back more than any other is their concern for how the recipient might receive this information, and particularly the emotional response that the subject matter may invoke.

Generally speaking, when faced with the question of whether to embark upon a courageous conversation, the answer should be yes, rather than no. Unless you are naturally a forceful leader, most people are more inclined to shy away from necessary courageous conversations than to initiate unnecessary courageous conversations. When we are considering a future event five P's can help us: ***"Prior Planning Prevents Poor Performance."*** When considering having a courageous conversation these five P's will help us make sure the conversation goes as well as it can. It will always be more successful to the extent that we have planned for it ahead of time.

Prior planning for a courageous conversation entails: 1. The gathering of all relevant facts; 2. Talking to other people about the situation and how the conversation might best be delivered and managed; and 3. Considering in advance the best possible courses of action you can take if the conversation doesn't go well and the issue

BEING FOREWARNED PRIOR TO A COURAGEOUS CONVERSATION IS TO BE FOREARMED.

remains unresolved. There is a military saying that, *'To be forewarned is to be fore-armed'*, and preparing for these conversations it is incredibly beneficial. The person initiating the courageous conversation needs to clearly understand the key focus and desired outcome, and needs to consider elements of the recipient's reaction or response which may be a deflection from the core content of the conversation. This phase of preparation is not to be under-estimated. It is the equivalent of being 'forewarned', which gives rise to the ability to be 'forearmed' with strategies to keep the conversation on track.

Teaching a Bold Dog New Tricks

Several years ago, I had a young leader on training who had a particularly resistant team member. This team member was very averse to change both in his private life and in his work life. This was a long-term characteristic in his life that showed up in examples such as bringing the exact same lunch to work every single day of the year, even if the company was putting on a special lunch that day. Although the team leader struggled with getting the team member to embrace change, the more significant issue was his attitude. He was negative about absolutely everything and in the team leader's own words, everyone walked on egg shells around this person.

During the training course, I encouraged the team leader to step up and address the team member's attitude – to have a courageous conversation. He was incredibly reluctant to do so because he was new in the position of leadership. Previous management had also been unwilling to address the resistant team member. He seemed like an impossible project. One of my simple philosophies in training and in life is; "The greater the challenge, the greater the reward." I knew that this was an opportunity for the team leader to experience growth both in his capability and in his confidence.

The goal for me in these situations where the person in leadership is new to the practice of courageous conversations, and lacks confidence, is simply that they *have* the conversation irrespective of the outcome of the conversation. That is a much simpler goal to achieve than seeing a positive conclusion come about as a result of tackling the issue head on. All I wanted this team leader to do was to actually have the conversation, something which he had been reluctant to do up to this point. It was about getting on the field and playing rather than winning, and when it comes to confidence and ability there is no substitute for quantity - the more of these conversations you attempt, the more your confidence (and competence) increases.

To be forewarned is to be forearmed so we did several role-plays with the team leader around how this conversation might play out using the facts of the case. We worked on ways to respond to possible deflections and defensiveness that might be part of the conversation. I'm sure that the team leader would have said that these made him feel more nervous rather than more confident, but I'm aware from years of experience that practicing and discussing the scenario in advance means that people may not feel any better, but they will be better equipped when it comes to actually having the conversation. When you ask others to help you prepare for a courageous conversation you also get the added bonus of sensing another's support as you step out to have the conversation. ***Knowing others are standing with you can make a big difference to your own sense of confidence.*** They can also help you fine tune your own demeanor and language to ensure you present in an appropriate manner.

In less than a week I received a phone call from the leader saying that he had had the conversation. It had gone far better than he could have imagined. As is so often the case with new leaders, their fear is greater than the reality of the situation. He called his team member in to address several issues which were going to mean major changes for the team member, including the fact that he would no longer get picked up for work every morning. On top of that he would have to change the vehicle that he had used every day for work for the previous ten years - something he was hugely opposed to. Finally, the team leader addressed his attitude because the rest of the team worked in constant fear of upsetting him.

The team member was clearly angered by the conversation to the point that, once all the issues were out on the table, he got up and walked out. An hour or so later he came back into the team leader's office and thanked him for having the courage to address these issues. He even went on to say that he was tired of being angry and how much it was detrimentally impacting his own family, as well as his work life. It was a response that the team leader never dreamed of receiving from someone who was so resistant. It was also a huge learning curve for the team leader because he had thought that this team member was incapable of change.

I was thrilled for the team leader but I was not overly surprised having seen similar scenarios play out in the same way over the years. When we got back together as a group the other participants were extremely complimentary of the team leader and of the outcome of the conversation. The key achievement for this leader though was not his skill in conversing in a way that allowed him to influence the staff member's life, fantastic as that was, but his greatest achievement was in mustering the courage to have the conversation in the first place.

When 'Hard Pressed' is a Good Thing

When leaders are struggling with having conversations with team members who aren't measuring up in terms of performance, behavior, or attitude I often use this illustration to encourage them. I will walk up to a piece of movable furniture such as a chair or a table and I'll push or lift the object. I'll then ask the participants to tell me what just happened. They typically reply; "You moved the table", or, "You lifted the chair." I then walk over to a wall, preferably an exterior wall, and then push against that with all my might, making it clear that I am making a lot of effort but not getting anywhere. I then ask the group the same question; "What just happened?" People generally reply; "Nothing." I then say that it appears as if nothing has happened but in fact, based on the principles of resistance training, whether I lifted the chair or pushed the table I exercised my muscles, and if I did that regularly they would become stronger and more capable. In the same manner when I push against an immovable object like a wall, even though it appears on the surface that nothing is happening, if I was to do it regularly enough I would get stronger over time.

Sometimes as leaders we can grow weary of constantly pushing against immovable objects. It is disheartening not to see a result for our hard work. The illustration demonstrates the fact that even though we may not shift a person, or get a positive result from a conversation, we still gain personal confidence from the experience, and the more of these conversations we have, the better we become at having them, and the readier we are to embark on them in the future.

Land of the Free and Home of the Brave

A number of common fears can hold us back from having necessary courageous conversations. We don't talk about these fears as much as we should, given that ***the ability to have courageous conversations would be one, if not the, most important leadership competencies***. The response that we fear the most from the person we have the courageous conversation with is usually a negative emotional response. It's helpful to consider what those negative emotional responses, or more accurately reactions, might be, and to consider how we might manage these.

Having considered what might happen and being somewhat prepared for the 'unexpected' makes us enter these conversations more confidently, and vastly increases our chances of positively influencing the person and the outcome. It can also be helpful to remind ourselves that if we approach the conversation in a professional and mature fashion with the intent of addressing the issue in a constructive manner, then the other person's reactions are their responsibility. If they react adversely then it often simply reinforces the issue that's being raised, and the necessity of addressing it.

CHANGING THE ATMOSPHERE

Many years ago, I had a CEO speak at a leadership program that I was delivering. He talked about effectively leading people. As part of his discussion he stated that two of the most powerful words that he uses in his leadership were 'disappointed' and 'proud'. He said that whenever possible, and appropriate, he would use the word 'proud' as the strongest word he knew to express gratitude and appreciation for what individual staff members or teams had achieved in terms of the business goals. Conversely, he would use the word 'disappointed' as the strongest word he knew to convey a message of dissatisfaction regarding ineffective or poor performance.

During later discussions with a group of saw mill workers, one of the course participants expressed how uncomfortable he was with the word 'proud' being used in the workplace setting. He stated that if his manager described being proud of a team member it would lessen the team's respect for him. He wasn't comfortable with a person in leadership expressing positive feelings towards a team member and went on to say, "What's next - a group hug?!?"

One of the attitudes I am always attempting to influence in workplace training is that of positivity. As the attendees had expressed only moderate levels of motivation at the beginning of the day I decided to wrap up the training by getting each participant to state what they thought were the strengths and positive attributes of the person to their right. Because we had had some banter throughout the day over the use of the word 'proud', when it came to this participant receiving feedback from another participant I was not surprised when the person on his left began by saying, "I feel really proud of this guy because...", (causing considerable laughter amongst the group). Once again in a risky move on my part, I walked to the back of the room where this participant was sitting and spread my arms out in a non-verbal invitation for a hug and was very surprised (and somewhat relieved truth be known) when he stood up and reciprocated my invitation to the delight and applause of everyone in attendance.

Don't get me wrong - I'm not on a personal crusade to get people to hug each other. I am, however, very determined to push people's boundaries in terms of seeing people change to become more positive and more responsible for creating positive cultures around about them. Of course, I'm not expecting that the guy who hugged me will start to hug his team members but I do believe his thought processes were challenged somewhat by the event and that he can now encourage himself to push things a little bit farther with his team for their sake and for the sake of the company.

Culture Shock

I worked with an organization one year that was quite different from me in nature. I am very extroverted and really enjoy humorous interaction. This organization, on the other hand, was relatively conservative and staffed by people who were quite introverted and serious in nature. I have been aware of the concept of a 'hidden culture' ever since I came across the term in my study for my business degree. Businesses or corporations have two cultures. The first is the culture that is stated in all its printed matter, and one that you are typically exposed to during the induction process. The second is hidden culture - one which you learn about over time by osmosis. It may be whispered about, but you're much more likely to observe it than hear about it directly. Hidden culture may even be in direct opposition to the organization's stated culture.

In my first few weeks of working within this organization I found myself talking to a fellow employee and asking them to describe the organization's culture, to which they answered; "I'm not exactly sure how to explain it, but one thing I can tell you is that it sure has changed since you've joined!" ***Much of the influencing we do with people is at a micro level.*** Most of our influence - with our children, partners, friends, neighbors, colleagues, and teammates – is happening through the small incremental day to day impacts of our words, behaviors and attitudes. But there are occasions when the issue or issues that need to be addressed and shifted are at a macro level and require a more macro approach. It can be a lot more work, and a lot more challenging, but the rewards are multiplied. It just takes a little courage!

CHAPTER ELEVEN

SELF INFLUENCE

"And why worry about a speck in your friend's eye
when you have a log in your own?
First get rid of the log in your own eye;
then you will see well enough to deal
with the speck in your friend's eye."
Jesus (NLT)

INTRODUCTION

Change and growth are often uncomfortable, but having self-control, setting yourself personal challenges that you rise to meet, and having heroes that you can look to as inspiring role models for influencing others, all help your own levels of credibility with others to increase. When people's trust in you increases, so does your ability to influence them. The first step to self-influence is self-awareness. When we are aware of how we are behaving, what we are thinking, and how we are feeling, we can then influence ourselves for change and betterment.

Show and Tell (not just 'Tell')

A while ago I found myself in a conversation with a severely obese gentleman. He noticed that I have a very controlled dietary regime and I am quite enthusiastic about physical exercise including competitive sports and resistance training. I found it somewhat odd when shortly after discovering these things about me he began to lecture me about the most effective dietary and exercise practices. He then told me that I needed to change my current diet and fitness regime to be more in line with his own thinking on the matter. I remember thinking how ironic it was that he was trying to influence me to change my diet and exercise methodology even though I was in pretty good shape for my age and he was unable to walk up a set of stairs without taking a breather half way up! Suffice to say his theory on Germanic dietary habits and Ecuadorian exercise principles had absolutely no influence on me whatsoever - in fact they had the opposite effect. His opinions only served to undermine his credibility in my eyes and made me doubt the validity of any of the information he was trying to impact me with.

11.1

BEING COMFORTABLE WITH BEING UNCOMFORTABLE

I am a strong believer that *the more you have been on a journey of self-discovery and self-improvement the more you will have the right to have influence in the lives of others*. Self-improvement, in its very nature, is going to make you a little uncomfortable at times. When we improve our diet, we may need to reduce our comfort eating. When we improve our fitness, we may need to reduce our comfort TV watching. Usually these changes are only a temporary discomfort as we quickly adjust and become comfortable in a new way of doing things.

The Power of Won

I once had a team leader in training who asked how to get people to do what you want them to do and how to get them to improve their performance when their attitude is somewhat apathetic. I asked her what the organization's values were and she replied that they weren't very clear but she wished that one of the values was "Excellence." I constantly enquire as to an organization's values because this is a very useful point to leverage off for improved performance in terms of setting the bar for behavior and attitude. It was therefore interesting to note that a significant portion of the next training day was due to highlight the organizational value of 'Excellence'. So, the next day, once we had concluded the content on excellence the rest of the group began to discuss how this leader might communicate and leverage off this value. She went away armed with enthusiasm and some great ideas for creating a culture of excellence in her team.

Sometime later I received correspondence from this leader saying that she had met some resistance from a team member to one of her ideas for celebrating and reinforcing excellence on an individual basis within the team. When I next saw this leader, I asked her, "What did you say to this resistant team member?" She replied; "I told her that I did not want to make her uncomfortable and that I understood the reason why she preferred not to participate."

One of my most repetitive sayings in leadership development is, "Comfort is the enemy of growth", and a saying that follows closely on its heels, "As a leader you need to be comfortable with feeling uncomfortable." So, I began my discussion with her by asking her:

"Remind me of your vision for your team?"

"Excellence in everything we do."

"And how will you go about that?" I asked?

"I want to celebrate and therefore reinforce small individual acts of excellence."

"So, having people feel comfortable isn't part of your vision for the team at all?"

"No" she replied.

Slowly it dawned on her that **she was allowing the team member's reaction to take precedence over her vision for the team.** Armed with some clear thinking over her role as a leader and the driver of team culture, she returned to have something of a 'showdown' with this team member. Shortly after I received an email from the team leader and I smiled broadly when I read the subject line, "I won!"

Often to influence others we may have to step outside our comfort zone and be comfortable with the discomfort of that. It may be necessary for us to draw people out of their comfort zones too in order to see change, particularly in order to achieve culture change in an organization. In the previous story, the leader felt uncomfortable with 'forcing' one of her team members to join the journey to excellence, and prior to talking to me she had allowed this team

COMFORT IS THE ENEMY OF GROWTH.

member's discomfort to dictate her vision for the team as a whole. People need to feel that their viewpoint is acknowledged by leadership, but discomfort with genuinely positive change is not reason enough to adhere to the status quo. The more we step outside our comfort zone, and encourage others to do the same, the more discomfort turns onto comfort.

In my younger years, I lacked confidence and ability in this area and my discomfort levels were very high, say 80% to 90%, and my comfort levels were conversely very low at 10% to 20%. The more situations that I've pushed myself into in terms of influencing others, the more the scales have swung increasingly towards comfort in these situations. I now have very little discomfort with confronting people with the need to change for their sake, but I had to journey through the early years of feeling incredibly uncomfortable with the process, particularly in early leadership roles. The old adage of "practice makes perfect" could be adjusted in this instance to more applicably read *"practice makes confident"*.

At the root of the discomfort that we sometimes feel is fear of rejection, fear of failure, and the fear of criticism. These fears can all be obstacles to doing what we need to do and saying what we need to say to influence people and shift the status quo. I've often said that everyone has insecurities, it's just how many we have and the extent to which we allow those insecurities to inhibit our functioning that counts. That's why, to be an influencer, we need to have a clear vision for why we want to influence someone else, and we need courage to step into that place of influence.

The Fear Factor

Being 'comfortable with feeling uncomfortable' is similar to bravery or courage, both of which are only ever required in direct correlation to the amount of anxiety or fear that's being felt. I remember leading an exercise with various groups that generated real anxiety amongst many of the participants. The participants had to approach an unsuspecting stranger on the street and generate a sales-based conversation with them. I told them that they couldn't afford to wait until the fear dissipated, as that would never happen, despite some of them thinking they needed to wait till their fear had calmed to begin the exercise. Fear is like a little 'add on' that you need to address, verbally if necessary, telling it that you are going ahead, whether it likes it or not. The fear can join you or stay at the door and leave you to get on with the activity, but regardless you are going ahead - with or without it.

This, in a nutshell, is being comfortable with being uncomfortable. The vast majority of participants attempted the task and found that firstly, the fear was not as crippling as they expected it to be once they determined to soldier on regardless, and secondly once they had experienced success, the fear would diminish (or at least their perspective of it would become more realistic) and with each successive success their fear or discomfort continued to abate.

Influencing people can be an uncomfortable process for both parties, but in order to grow in our ability to effectively influence others there will be many times when it is necessary to live with discomfort, and face our fears, during the process. If you are going to be an influencer - ***get comfortable with being uncomfortable***!

INFLUENCING BY EXAMPLE

It's not always possible to influence people simply by role modelling and demonstrating a better way, but it can sometimes be enough to effect change on its own. At the very least ***role modelling must be congruent with the messages being communicated***, because hypocrisy is a great way to achieve the opposite of what you're after.

Throwing an Alternative

In football, much like rugby, when the ball goes out it is a throw-in to the opposing team. Although there should be an advantage to throwing the ball in, it often ends up being not much more likely than 50-50 odds that the throwing team will maintain possession. For years I've been perplexed by the way that football teams take throw ins. The player will leave the pitch to retrieve the ball, come walking casually back to the line at the edge of the field and then start to think about where they will throw the ball. Meanwhile both their own team's players and the opposition have plenty of time to take up positions to thwart the thrower's advantage in having the ball.

There are two things that I do differently. The first is that I act quickly and will often throw the ball in several meters even before I return to the edge of the pitch. My own players can be quite surprised by this initially despite me warning them repeatedly that this is my practice. Certainly, the opposition are most surprised and therefore it means that we tend to win more than 80% of possession from my throw ins - quite a significant percentage increase from the normal method. The second factor that makes these throw-ins so useful is that I will often throw backwards from where the ball went out, often to our own unmarked players, which invariably means that we get 100% possession and can continue to play the ball on the ground rather than in the air.

Many years ago when I joined a new football team I did not expressly talk to them about my two different strategies for throwing the ball in, but by the time I had played with them for three or four games I noticed that were also doing the same thing without me even articulating that it is a really successful strategy. It would have felt inappropriate to try and verbally influence them at that early stage, but simply by demonstrating its effectiveness, people began to catch on and replicate the practice. Sometimes actions really do speak louder than words!

Bully for You!

I attended teachers' training through an extramural program with a tertiary institution. We had limited contact with lecturers via assignment and practical work but occasionally they would come and visit us on-site. I was on my final practicum in a school with a very good-natured senior teacher supervising me. As coincidence would have it, when my lecturer came to visit me on-site, my senior teacher recognized her as soon as she entered the room, although she didn't let on at any point that she remembered her.

After she left I found out that my senior teacher had known the lecturer many years previously having gone to the same high school together, and the lecturer had badly bullied her during those years. You can imagine how my perspective on the lecturer changed when I found out that the person who was responsible for equipping me to look after children had actually been a perpetrator of bullying! How embarrassed she must have felt meeting one of her ex-victims in such a professional setting! What must my senior teacher have thought of this lecturer because of their previous history? Obviously, it is impossible to turn the clock back and erase the mistakes that we've made in our younger days, but I've often wondered if this lecturer recognized her victim, and if she had, what must have gone through her mind? Our ability to influence others, particularly those that we are in relationship with, is a sum total of their experience of us. The examples we have created over the years will build a story in our lives of whether or not people can trust us over the long term. Treat people well and your influence with them will increase. Treat them poorly and it will decrease.   Our actions either build trust and increase our deposits into people's 'Relational Bank Accounts' or they decrease trust and deplete the good will.

A Foul Weather Friend

When I was growing up I was too busy playing football and tennis and working part-time jobs to do any reading. Some people love reading but for me it was simply a chore that occasionally had to be performed for the sake of school work. I've had to push myself to be a reader as an adult but that push has been immensely beneficial and enjoyable. At the beginning of 2016 I realized that I had not read many biographies, so I set myself a goal to read as many biographies as I could. This was a hugely rewarding experience.

For years I have admired Ernest Shackleton and had been meaning to get around to reading his story, and my goal afforded me the opportunity to do just that. Ernest Shackleton is probably now better remembered (and admired), not for his failed crossing of Antarctica, but for his epic leadership in ultimately bringing his entire expedition crew safely back to England.

The story tells of Shackleton and his crew being forced to abandon their ship in the Antarctic to be crushed by the ice pack. They eventually made their way in lifeboats to Elephant Island, which is located between Antarctica and their target destination of the South Georgia Island whaling station. After some time stranded on the island they realized that there was very little hope of being rescued and so Shackleton determined to put out in one of the lifeboats with a small crew to make their way to the whaling station and bring a ship back to rescue the rest of the crew.

Obviously, with very limited places available in the lifeboat it was vitally important that Shackleton took people with relevant skills such as navigation and carpentry. However, he made a fascinating leadership decision to take an additional crew member who not only had no relevant skills for the journey, but was in fact Shackleton's least favorite crewmember who was universally disliked by the entire party. It was for this specific reason that Shackleton decided to include him in their small sailing party. He believed that if he left the crew member on the island with the bulk of the crew he would continue to demoralize the entire group and jeopardize their survival. Therefore, Shackleton made the decision to take this crew member and bear the burden of his company himself rather than leave the burden for the remainder of the crew on Elephant Island.

This is a tremendous example of sacrificing the needs of the few for the sake of the many, and living out your leadership values in the real world. It is true professionalism and is one of several factors that caused Shackleton to be so well admired and respected by his men. He was truly a gifted leader who understood human relationships and knew how to use his influence to get the best possible outcome, even at his own expense. *When we strengthen our ability to influence our self through managing our own behaviors, thoughts and attitudes, we strengthen our ability to influence others.*

It's All Fun and Games Till Someone Loses Their Ideal

Once when I was delivering a leadership program for frontline leaders I had genuine concerns about the attitude of one of the participants. He was an incredibly likeable character, but he obviously struggled to know where to draw the line between having fun and the need to maintain a professional persona.

It came to my attention on the second day of the program that this young man had been on another training program where his sense of humor had gotten the better of him resulting in the facilitator laying a formal written complaint about him. Someone handed me an iPad so I could read the letter of complaint in front of the group participants. Using real-life and timely situations as examples in my training is incredibly powerful. They provide an opportunity to examine people's genuine attitudes and behavior and potentially make a meaningful difference to their leadership journey and to their lives as a whole. This situation related directly to the young man's ability and future as a leader.

The other group members treated the letter as something of a joke to begin with. Some of the participants became somewhat defensive of the young man until they could see that I was genuinely interested in impacting his leadership journey. I told them that if we focused on the faults or the character flaws of the facilitator who laid the complaint, then the young man who was the center of the complaint would miss an opportunity for learning and growth in his own journey. He would miss the opportunity to grow in his 'Above the Line' responses if he was allowed to continue unchecked with 'Below the Line' responses such as defensiveness and lack of ownership.

As we discussed the issue further the young man began to take responsibility for his attitude and seemed to come to a genuine realization that it was time for him to reconsider the way that he conducted himself with his team and also with external clients and suppliers. It was a seminal moment for him and we could all see that his leadership journey would now be defined in terms of BE and AE: "before that email" and "after the email". In this case, personal awareness and self-leadership changed his life for the better.

Eat, Drink and be Very (Early to Leave)

As a new leader, we often need to exhibit some degree of professional distance from people we now lead who were once in our peer group. This can be an uncomfortable part of the leadership journey – redefining roles and friendships - but to be effective as a leader I must increasingly become comfortable with being uncomfortable.

I once ran a leadership course where we were fortunate enough to have Steve Maharey (the ex– New Zealand Minister of Education and Vice Chancellor of Massey University) speak on the topic of leadership. The participants were in middle management roles and as such it was good to have someone from such a high-level position of leadership come and address us, as well as being invaluable to hear about Maharey's experience as a cabinet minister.

Maharey told us that he very rarely attended social occasions with his staff but if he did attend he would never be the last person to leave, and indeed is often the first. At these public social occasions, he also had a personal rule to never have more than one or two drinks. Obviously, Maharey's time as a senior politician had a part to play in his awareness of the media, and consequently the public's perception of him. Now that he is much less in the public eye he still has a keen awareness of his need to maintain a professional persona. He talked to us about the need to *maintain professional distance between yourself as a leader and the team that you are leading*. Maharey said that it's not appropriate, or even easy, to go out drinking and enjoying a good time with staff on a Friday night, and then find yourself needing to discipline a staff member on Monday morning. Obviously, the participants on the leadership course had nowhere near the same level of public profile as Maharey had but still there was pertinent wisdom in his message to always maintain a degree of professionalism. This is the 'loneliness' that some leaders speak of, particularly when they first transition from being 'one of the team' into 'the leader of the team'.

(Slightly) Old School

I remember in a less lofty fashion, but in a similar vein, being interviewed for a primary teacher's position. Although this was my first job as a qualified teacher, I was in my mid-thirties and had had numerous employment roles by that stage. I was asked by a Board member during the interview, "How will you get on in terms of being a friend of the children?" I replied: "It's my job to be friendly, but I certainly don't aim to be their friend." That answer seemed to more than satisfy the inquirer and the interview moved on to other matters.

When teachers are too friendly with children, particularly younger teachers in their first position, their professional standards can be compromised, and in turn their ability to have influence with the children diminishes. The same thing happens when leaders in the workplace don't maintain healthy boundaries with their subordinates. The chain of command becomes blurred and influence can ultimately be compromised.

11.3

PERSONAL AWARENESS

Taking personal responsibility for our lives is a key factor in self-influence. In order to influence our self, we need to ***recognize that we are in charge of our self***. We can't 'pass the buck' to anyone else to be responsible for our life once we reach adulthood. One of the reasons we don't take responsibility for our actions and attitudes is that we are unaware of them. We all have areas of our life that, for whatever reason, we don't see. There are things about every one of us that are only known by us. We are the ones who know our thoughts, dreams and true desires more than anyone else. Many of these things we will share with others, but sometimes there are ideals and aspirations that we have never really become conscious of ourselves. While these things may be out of sight, and even out of mind, they are not out of action in terms of influencing us.

One way we can 'self-influence' is to reflect on our thoughts, behaviors, feelings and attitudes. Taking time to write things down can serve to clarify our own understanding of ourselves. If we are willing to listen to others in order to understand their perspective, we should also be willing to listen to our self! In our busy lives, we tend to underestimate the benefits of taking time to think. We rarely debrief our own behavior by processing it through personally. Yet this trait has been identified as one of the traits of great leaders and influencers.

Warren Buffett, CEO of one of the largest businesses in America, stated that he spent 80% of his career reading and thinking. Bill Gates, one of the most successful influencers in the world, is said to take two weeks off each year to spend time thinking deeply without interruption. Jeff Weiner, the CEO of LinkedIn, allocates two hours every working day just for reflection and thought. We are sometimes so busy working that we neglect the most important things! As Abraham Lincoln said, "Give me six hours to chop down a tree and I will spend the first four sharpening the axe."

As well as self-reflection, having others speak into our lives can help us to understand the things we don't see in ourselves. We can all benefit from the perspectives of 'trusted others'. Other people can see things we overlook. ***What do others see about us that we have missed?*** Just as an editor picks up spelling and grammatical errors that the writer has not noticed in their intent on getting their work done, other people can often easily spot those things we haven't noticed about ourselves. On the flip side, other people can help us to see the positive things about our self that we may have overlooked, underestimated, or neglected. The key is to find people who genuinely care about you, and who you trust, to gain their perspective. With both self-reflection and other people's reflection, kindness is the path to change.

CHAPTER TWELVE

WHOLE BODY COMMUNICATION

"The most important thing in communication
is hearing what isn't said."
Peter Druker

INTRODUCTION

Communicating well involves a high degree of self-awareness and 'other-awareness'. One of the ways we can increase our personal self-awareness, and our awareness of others, is through noticing our physical reactions and expressions, and those of others around us. Communication is a key component in the process of influencing others, and as we are aware, communication clearly involves more than just verbalized language. The three key elements of communication are: body language (including facial expression), tone of voice (the intonation of our words – the way in which we are speaking), and the actual words that we use.

It's All in the Genes!

In my training, I often use this example to illustrate the power of body language and vocal tone. Imagine that my wife and I getting ready to go out to dinner and as she comes walking into the bathroom she asks me how she looks in her new jeans. In reply I look very nervous and begin to scratch my neck. My face becomes etched with guilt and discomfort. Despite this my reply is a simple, "Good", with no inflection in my voice. By this point the participants in the training room are laughing and I say, "You think I'm on the couch tonight?" To which they commonly respond, "You're on the couch for the whole week mate!"

So instead I alter the scenario slightly. I suggest that my wife asks me how she looks in her new jeans as she walks through the bathroom - but this time she's made it into the bedroom before she hears my reply. I will walk around to the back of a whiteboard to simulate my wife being unable to see me, and once again I reply, "Good", but this time in a very high-pitched and nervous sounding tone. This again causes laughter in the room and comments regarding how permanent my stay on the couch might become. I ask the participants what I've done wrong because the word that I used once again is 'good' and my wife couldn't see my body language at all. Naturally the participants reply that although my body language cannot be seen this time, my tone is far from convincing.

When our body language and our tone are incongruent with the words that we are speaking, *people will accept the dominant message from our non-verbal communication* as opposed to the words that we speak.

Watch Your Mouth!!
(and Your Eyes… and Your Hands… and Your Tone…)

"Watch your attitude - everyone else is!" You may have heard that non-verbal communication makes up the bulk of all communication. Research by Albert Mehrabian determined that non-verbal communication makes up 93% of our communication with another person, with body language making up 55%, and tone making up 38%. This discovery was made while observing conversations which were in some way emotive, such as those involving a contentious topic – so these statistics may not apply across all communication situations. Regardless, 93% in any situation is staggeringly high and means that when we are involved in emotionally charged communication with someone, then regardless of the words we speak, the overwhelming message will be conveyed via our body language and particularly via our facial expressions.

Parenting expert Ian Grant had a favorite saying; "Children are great perceivers but not necessarily great interpreters." A child might easily perceive that something is wrong with mum or dad because of an inflection in their tone of voice, or an unusual look on their face, but have more difficulty interpreting why they have that tone of voice or what has caused that look on their face. When we don't understand the full context, voice tone or body language may be interpreted completely incorrectly.

In the same way, as adults, we may read people and perceive attitudes that aren't there, or worse, perceive attitudes that are there that we are not aware of. For instance, if I am feeling frustrated during an interaction I need to be cognizant that I'm feeling agitated, and unless I want to come across in such a fashion, then I need to take control over my body language and my tone so that I'm confident they are not expressing agitation.

ATTITUDE AND ACTIONS

The generally held conception is that our body language and tone will reflect our attitude. Professor Amy Cuddy has discovered in her research that the opposite is also possible. Our body language can impact our attitude. In her experiments, Professor Cuddy took blood samples of participants and measured their testosterone and cortisol levels. She then got half of the subjects to strike very strong and dominant poses, such as having their hands behind their head and their feet up on a table, and the other half of the subjects to adopt very meek and mild poses, such as sitting hunched forward with their heads down. To test whether the poses had any impact on people's attitudes, Cuddy and her researchers measured people's propensity to take a risk both before and after striking the two types of poses by giving them simple opportunities to take risk via gambling.

What Cuddy discovered was that in those people who adopted very meek and mild poses their propensity to take a risk during the gambling activities dropped, as did their testosterone levels (an assertiveness inducing hormone) whilst their cortisol levels (a stress modulating hormone) increased. The opposite occurred in those who struck very strong poses. These participants had an increase in their propensity to take a gambling risk, and following the striking of these poses their testosterone levels increased while cortisol levels decreased. The

CHANGING YOUR BODY LANGUAGE CAN CHANGE YOUR MIND!

upshot of Cuddy's research is that our attitude can be physically influenced by our conscious body language.

To some degree, you can choose your mood. If you are feeling particularly frustrated or angry then try putting a huge smile your face for several seconds and observe just how much your internal attitude shifts because of your dramatic change in countenance. If you are feeling intimidated or depressed, shift your posture to a strong upright position. If you are feeling stuck – try going for a run. We know now that *simply changing our body language can help shift our feelings and thinking.*

Could You Use a Lift??

I was talking with a New Zealand counsellor who does a lot of work with the parents of pre-schoolers. He specialized in working with parents with anger issues. He would invariably give them this advice: when they found themselves unable to control their anger, they were to raise their eyebrows as high as they could. Give this a try yourself some time. It is almost impossible to remain in a heated state whilst raising your eyebrows as high as they'll possibly go. I'm sure that this has something to do with the fact that we feel somewhat silly having our eyebrows unusually elevated! However, the counsellor shared with me the science behind this strategy. There is a small gland in the brain which, when the eyebrows are raised, secretes a hormone which causes us to relax. We are such complex creatures that virtually our every action has multiple and diverse consequences. *When we aim for positive actions and behaviors we can expect to see multiple subsequent positive consequences!*

Don't Roll Your Eyes at Me!

Dr John Gottman and his research team observed numerous couples having a three-minute conversation on a somewhat contentious and unresolved issue. They then tracked these couples over years, and eventually decades, to observe which couples divorced, and what these couples did differently from those couples who didn't later divorce. Gottman and his research team discovered that, among many other interesting observations, eye rolling, by one or both of the partners, but in particular by the husband, during the three-minute interaction, was somewhat surprisingly a common correlator with divorce.

It took the researchers additional time and study to determine that the presence of eye rolling was an indicator of an attitude of contempt. The researchers found that when women use eye rolling it is often not a sign of contempt but rather an attempt to soften the conversation with humor. So really – what they were observing in the body language was a toxic element of contempt - and men and women display this contempt in slightly different ways. A small, seemingly harmless physical expression was communicating a much deeper attitudinal issue. In the same way, small, seemingly inconsequential physical expressions on the positive spectrum can influence outcomes positively.

ALIGNING WORDS AND DEEDS

While body language is a large factor in our communication, words also play an important role. Our words and our body language need to ultimately align to avoid sending mixed messages. While we can try our best to make our body language communicate more positively than our thoughts might be thinking, no human has enough energy to keep this up indefinitely. It is far easier to 'self-influence' our thoughts so that they actually line up with what we would like our body to be expressing.

Mock Trial

In younger days, I picked up on the mocking habit of using the word 'awesome' to describe just about everything and anything good. I would use it with an American accent in a somewhat sarcastic tone (highly inappropriate, I know). The thing that I found fascinating was the more that I used it the more it became drained of any sense of negative connotations. The word itself was so positive and inspiring that over time it became part of my everyday vernacular and I couldn't help but using it in a positive way. As a result, I find myself to this day using it relatively frequently to positively describe people's behavior or situations. Despite being embarrassed to say that I ever used that word in the derisive manner, it was a fascinating experience to have the nature of the word and my attitude towards it change over time with its consistent use.

When I realized the power of such a positive word to change my attitude, I decided to try this exercise out with another word. I started adding the word 'brilliant' to my everyday vernacular also. It's not something that I'm entirely comfortable using yet, and certainly I'm a long way off from it being an automatic response when something goes well, but I'm committed to the journey of having another superlative join my vocabulary, and more importantly have it assist my attitude in being more positive.

We all inhabit a body and whether we know it or not we are constantly communicating to others through that body. In the process of influencing others, it's not enough to get our words just right. We must be cognizant of our internal attitude and perspective and be aware that our internal world can so easily seep out through our tone, our body language, and especially through our facial expressions. Effective influencers align attitude, non-verbal communication, and their words, to have the most positive impact possible on their audience. Great influencers are great self-influencers!

CHAPTER THIRTEEN

THE SOFTER SIDE

"How did you do that?" said the Wind.
"It was easy," said the Sun, "I lit the day.
Through gentleness I got my way."
Aesop's Fable

INTRODUCTION

It goes without saying that influence can be achieved by strong and even forceful means and still have a positive outcome for all parties concerned. However, there is a lot to be said for the power of a softer approach as alluded to in the quote above from Aesop's fable. In this story, there is a competition between the sun and the wind as to who can remove a gentleman's jacket first. The wind tries in vain to blow it off him with an aggressive approach, but the sun's warm manner makes it the ultimate victor. It is interesting to note that not only does the wind fail to coerce the man to remove his coat, but the opposite effect occurs with the man clutching more tightly to keep his coat on.

HUMILITY, VULNERABILITY AND KINDNESS

Having worked in corporates for many years I am pleased to see an increasing shift towards greater humility among senior leaders. It has always been easier to admire a humble leader than an arrogant leader, and this principle carries over into the influence of others. People are more open to the influence of people who act with humility than those who are egotistical. Vulnerability, humility, transparency and positivity are powerful ingredients to warm people to our influence.

I remember coming across a short article entitled, "Everything I needed to know in life to be successful I learnt at kindergarten." Although this article was somewhat tongue-in-cheek, the author's premise was that the behaviors we learn as children about socializing well with others – sharing, being considerate, being kind – were all vital ingredients for doing well relationally as an adult. Being a leader means being in relationships – albeit unique kinds of relationships – with others. ***When we invest kindness into these relationships we build up currency for future influence*** with those people.

Wherever I Go, I Know Egos

I was contracted to speak to a group of medical professionals at their annual conference on the subject of improved staff relations. The facts of the matter were that they had a much higher staff turnover than the national average. Coupled with this quantitative measure were several consistently occurring qualitative factors, such as comments from the staff that did not paint a very positive picture of work relations. As a non-medical speaker at the conference I was one of only a very small minority of session speakers whose name did not end in 'PhD', not to mention that I was the first and only speaker to address 'soft skills' issues. It was intimidating to say the least.

One of the aspects that I addressed was that of receiving feedback from those we are in authority over. This can be very difficult to do if our egos are less than receptive. It was a sensitive subject to broach with an already daunting audience, but if I didn't mention it then I felt I wouldn't have been adding as much value to the attendees and to the company as was possible.

Rather than telling people off or ostracizing them by merely instructing them to work differently, I chose to be vulnerable and share something of my own journey. I talked about how I had built a fierce ego of my own over the years, partly out of necessity, and partly to compensate for areas of personal inadequacy. Growing up without a father, and with a mother who struggled to function for years after his death, I unconsciously made the decision at a young age to forge a very independent path for myself. I was on my own in the world and I was going to survive it whatever way I could. I got my first paid job at the tender age of 10 years old, and I was thrilled to have my own disposable income. I spent my spare time from then on playing football and earning money.

On one occasion, in my final year of school, I was pulled into the high school principal's office. The principal wanted to know why I was continually late to school, to which I simply shrugged my shoulders. He said that he had heard that I was working part-time at a fast food chain and he asked me how much I worked. I replied that the hours varied. "How much did you work last week?" He asked. I sat there and calculated it in my head and then answered him: "36 hours." He was absolutely flabbergasted, and not knowing where to take the conversation from there he simply dismissed me by saying, "Well… try to be on time for school!"

I wouldn't listen to anyone's advice. In fact, more than that, I managed to foster the kind of thinking that would always oppose the status quo. So, when people discussed the daily news in my school class I would find myself constantly acting as the devil's advocate and voicing any oppositional opinion, regardless of how illogical it was. I was also immensely proud of my ability to 'think outside the square' and to consider factors that others had overlooked. How foolish I was! Little did I realize at the time that I was setting myself up for poor future relationships with my contempt and arrogance. I was the king of contempt, and contempt is the poison of relationships.

I told the attendees at the conference that it is important that we have a *healthy* ego, but I know what it's like to have an overzealous ego. A self-centered ego can do me, and those around me, considerable disservice, let alone damage.

At one point during my presentation I told the attendees, "I brought my ego with me. No doubt many of you brought yours with you also. I've got mine in my bag, I'll show it to you!" As I reached into my bag I then lifted my head and added, "Now you know that egos are invisible, don't you?!? So, what I'll actually show you is my 'EMS' - my Ego Management System", and out from my bag I lifted a solid dog leash with a muzzle attached." I then went on to talk about my ego being important to my well-being as a young child having to survive a tragic situation, but that very same ego had become destructive in many of my relationships over the years. Hence, I now keep it on a leash with a muzzle to stop it from attacking others (and even from attacking me at times!).

In this situation *I used honesty and vulnerability to broach a very sensitive subject*, sharing something of my own story and experience to 'soften the landing' of an issue that had the potential to be very confrontational. I was pleased when no one walked out of the session and even more pleased that the audience seemed genuinely receptive to this challenging topic!

The Most (Self) Absorbent Product on the Market

Vulnerability isn't always the most appropriate approach to take when attempting to influence people. I have seen on many occasions people make too much of an effort to be vulnerable in an attempt to relate and connect. Often that mistake is more an indication of lack of experience or confidence than true humility.

On one occasion in my journey to discovering the value of vulnerability, I made an appointment to see a counsellor. I had never seen this counsellor before. I was hoping I would gain some new insights into my own behavior but instead I went home from the appointment pondering on the fact that the counsellor had spent more time speaking about himself than about the reason for my being there. I was so surprised by just how much he had talked about himself that I made a quick mental note about the number of distinct stories he had told from his own background. I calculated that he told 25 of his own sto-

personal stories in a 60-minute appointment! Aside from a brief introduction, he didn't find out anything about my situation in his own efforts to lecture me from his own experience.

When I spoke to him later I told him I wouldn't be rebooking another appointment with him, and explained that it was because I felt like he talked more about himself than he did about the issues I was paying him to help me with. At this he became defensive and rationalized that he had simply been trying to connect with me by talking about unrelated stories from his own life. His desire to be vulnerable in an attempt to connect was plausible, but it had the opposite effect in terms of influencing me. What I needed (and what I was paying for) was his expertise in terms of my presenting issue, and by inappropriately opening up to me about so many of his own struggles he had actually undermined his credibility with me and I chose not to engage his services again. There is a time and place for personal vulnerability.

What Right Don't You Have

Vulnerability is a powerful means for influencing others. There are times when the most useful tools for influencing people may be passion or assertiveness. However, there are other times when humility and vulnerability may be more appropriate vehicles to shift the thinking and behavior of others. ***Vulnerability has the effect of bridging the gap between people.***

At one time, I worked alongside a fellow facilitator who in days gone by had represented New Zealand in their field of physical endeavor. For the several years that I had known this man he had been exemplary in maintaining a high level of physical fitness. What sur-

surprised me was that he never talked about his physical discipline when he was training others. When I questioned him on it he said that he didn't feel like he had the right to tell people how to be as fit as he was, given how excellent he had been in his sport. He didn't want to appear arrogant or intimidating. I find it fascinating that someone like myself who has never physically competed at a national level, and who has nothing particularly special to give me credibility to speak on this topic, may have more confidence to influence in this area than someone with much more experience and ability.

If I am too far ahead of people, as was the case with the ex-New Zealand sporting representative, then I may be able to increase people's ability to connect with me by talking about an area of vulnerability I have, such as struggling with weight gain once I stopped competing at elite level. That kind of ***honesty is attractive to people*** and can sometimes have a greater influence than being a distant and unrelatable super role model. Conversely, when people are 'ahead of me', such as the attendees at the medical conference who were all much more qualified than I am, then I can use vulnerability to admit that I'm not perfect in one or more areas, and this can have the effect of people coming and 'sitting with me where I'm at'. Both scenarios utilize vulnerability to draw people closer together, building connection and trust in the relationship, thus increasing the chance of influence occurring.

It is worth noting that vulnerability must be genuine. It is not a tool to manipulate people into taking influence from you, but it is one of the methods by which connection is made and trust is built, and this trust is what enhances influence. ***When vulnerability is not genuine*** *people quickly discern this* and it will actually lead to reduced trust and correspondingly reduced influence.

THE POWER OF NICENESS

The "Dunedin Study" is a massive, longitudinal study of humankind based out of Dunedin, New Zealand. It is, in fact, the largest and longest of its kind in the world. Since 1972 this university research project has tracked every child born that year on an ongoing, annual basis. Unless people have passed away in the 40+ years that the research has been conducted, every single person is interviewed and tested every single year. They are funded by the study to return to Dunedin every year and if they are unable to return due to health reasons, or being incarcerated, then the researchers will go to them to maintain the robustness of the research data. The anonymity of the participants has been maintained into the fifth decade of the project, which is understandable given the personal depth of some of the questions including whether people have been involved in the sale of class 'A' drugs, or in violent crime.

One aspect of the Dunedin study which I find so incredibly interesting is that due to the depth and longevity of the study, the researchers are now able to pinpoint the kind of factors that lead to people's success in life including their success in work, finances and asset accumulation, and relationships. When I ask my leadership training participants what they think the two biggest contributing factors are towards people achieving success in life, seldom are people able to identify one factor and no one has ever identified both unless they are familiar with the study. ***The two factors that the study has identified that significantly lead to success are having the characteristics of 'agreeableness' and 'self-control'.***

Both agreeableness and self-control relate strongly to the process of influencing people. If I lack the ability to control myself then I am less likely to remain cognizant of the bigger picture when attempting to persuade people to shift. Lacking self-control in interactions may also result in the other party respecting us less, which will impact their trust in us. If we fail to control our emotions or our response, we even risk ultimately losing trust in ourselves. Agreeableness is a personality trait evident in individual behavioural characteristics such as kindness, sympathy, cooperativeness, warmth and consideration of others. These are the factors that help us to get along with others. These are the characteristics that help us achieve "Above the Line" responses.

Agree to Agree!

I ran a one day refresher course six months after delivering a leadership training block to a group of managers. As part of the refresher days I like to solicit stories of change, and one participant talked about how he had been attempting to be less argumentative. Naturally once he started aligning his behavior towards his goal he also started getting on better with people and finding that they were more open to his ideas. I talked with the group about how counterintuitive this can feel. We argue with people because we believe that we are right and they need to be influenced to see things from our (right) perspective. However, being opinionated and argumentative has the opposite effect with most

most people. ***No one wants to trust their heart to someone who shows contempt for it.*** They become turned off to our influence and can become defensive or just simply 'tune out' to our ideas. Conversely, being nice opens many doors that belligerent arguing finds well and truly locked. For this manager, it was a welcome surprise to find that once he stopped arguing with people in his family and workplace, they began to listen to him and respond to his thoughts and ideas much more actively.

Better to Give Than to Relieve

On one course I ran I had a 'hostage' in my leadership training. This gentleman was clearly unhappy that his time was being wasted covering content that he already knew and that, in his mind, was irrelevant to his job anyway. One of the ways that I have been attempting to improve my training over the last couple of years is to have less confectionery and more healthy food on the tables. I noticed that more and more people were commenting that I had brought fruit along for myself for morning tea when often all the participants had to eat were cakes and biscuits and sausage rolls. So, I started to bring a lot more fruit so that those who were more healthily inclined could eat as well as I do.

On this particular day, this 'hostage' (who had been softening as the course progressed) informed me that his wife was in Fiji on holiday and as he rushed to sort his lunch that morning without her help he comforted himself in the fact that "Sharkey would bring extra fruit" and he would be looked after! It was interesting to see just how much his attitude towards the course softened when it was helped along by the simple act of generosity, kindness and thoughtfulness.

On the final day of the course we were discussing relationships and I said to the group that - in an effort to build better friendships - I was starting to phone some of my male friends to simply ask how they were going. I also talked about wanting to make the effort to do this with my son who was living and attending university in another city at the time. When I suggested the idea of phoning a friend just to ask how things were going, the hostage boldly exclaimed, "No one asks people how they're going just for the sake of it! If I asked my son I'd get ignored or at best get a two-word reply!" So I challenged him to give it a try, suggesting that he really had nothing to lose.

The 'hostage' came back after morning tea shaking his head and saying that he couldn't believe what had just happened. He had accepted the challenge that I had given him and texted his son just simply to ask how he was going. He was astonished when he quickly received such a long answer to such a simple question that the reply took up two full text messages! *It doesn't take a lot to show an interest in people and simply be nice.* The results can be quite outstanding!

BEING NICE OPENS MANY DOORS THAT BELLIGERENT ARGUING FINDS WELL AND TRULY CLOSED.

Turning the Tables

One time I arrived at a new business to deliver training. I quickly observed that the training room in their facility had inadequate seating and table space. The manager that I was liaising with led me down to the lunch room and helped me lift out a lone table to use to make up the table space. While we were doing this, he was questioned - almost aggressively - by one of the office staff regarding taking the only lunch table staff had to eat off. The manager told the staff member that there was no other option and we carried the table to the training room while he watched on sullenly.

I delivered the day's training, and some of the participants returned the table back to the lunchroom. The second day of training a month later meant the same circumstance - having to take the table out of the lunchroom under the watchful gaze of the very same staff member who was still not at all happy with the arrangement.

Over the first few months of training I would encounter this upset staff member several times a day and I engaged him in conversation as I do with anyone that I meet in a new work environment. After some time he thawed out and we became friendly with each other to the point where he began to assist me with carrying the table out when I needed it. When I would arrive on site this staff member was usually the only other staff member in the building at the time, and when he would spot me coming down the corridor he would scoot out of his office to help me with the table.

It became more and more obvious that he was primarily coming out to have a friendly talk because I made a point, as I do generally in my conversations, to ask him several questions about himself to see how he was doing. ***It was niceness that turned his attitude around*** towards me to the point that he was willing to help me with a task that he vehemently disagreed with initially.

ACKNOWLEDGING THE VALUE OF OTHERS

There are times when passion and assertiveness and even forceful-ness get the job done in terms of influencing other people, however assertive and even forceful behavior should be used very sparingly. *People are highly motivated to maintain control of their own lives* and when they are forced into action motivation declines rapidly. There really is no substitute for treating people well with kindness and plain old niceness, and giving them the respect and value they each deserve as unique individuals.

Encouragement Motivates Loyalty

Having grown up without a primary male role model has made me a keen observer of the way fathers and grandfathers relate to children and grandchildren. One of the things I've noticed with grandparents in particular is that grandchildren will too often gravitate towards the soft and accepting grandmother in preference to the gruff and une-motional grandfather. I've had something of a goal over the years to try to become the kind of grandfather that my grandchildren just as easily approach as they do their grandmother. Absolutely crucial to this happening is my practice of kindness, acceptance and encour-agement!

My father-in-law has been an invaluable role model in this sense. Contrary to anything I witnessed growing up in my own wider family or amongst my friends' parents, he is remarkably calm under pressure, and harsh words are never heard exiting his mouth. He is always encouraging and never one bit derogatory with his humor. As

As a result, every one of his many grandchildren love spending time with him and absolutely adore him. These grandchildren take his influence readily. As the Dunedin study so accurately discovered, people who are agreeable get on better with others than people who aren't, and as a result are able to have more influence with those around them.

Lowering the Bar

A topic that I am passionate about is encouraging and equipping people to have better working relationships with those they lead. There is some very conclusive research evidence that shows that people's motivation correlates to the amount of recognition they receive. ***People need and want to be acknowledged for their work and contribution,*** and our businesses fare better when we pay attention to those needs and wants!

As human beings, we naturally crave recognition even for the work that is BAU - business as usual. When I'm commended for doing my job - even though I am naturally expected to do my job - it encourages me to go the extra mile even under difficult circumstances. When I don't receive basic appreciation for my general contribution it's much harder for me to put in the extra effort, because I may be concerned that it won't be recognized or rewarded. No-one wants to be invisible to others. We all find meaning and satisfaction in our work being of importance to someone else.

Knowing how important acknowledgement is to motivation, we can't really set the bar too high for praise. In the same way that we really appreciate being enthusiastically commended for doing what we are paid for, so too those we lead, who are just as human as we are, would also really appreciate such praise.

One of the things that helps us to set the praise bar low is to *be prepared to use superlatives* such as 'fantastic', 'awesome', 'great job' and 'brilliant work'. In the first instance this may seem above and beyond the effort that is being commended, but when you appreciate people for their effort, they tend to do even better next time and live up to that high standard you are setting anyway.

This process may be uncomfortable initially but as we know by now - people in leadership roles need to be increasingly comfortable with feeling uncomfortable. Not only is it okay but it is a very profitable to use superlatives even when the effort that has been delivered may not be 100% brilliant or 100% fantastic. If we are prepared to 'prime the pump' by using superlatives when the work performed may not quite justify them, then we are more likely to get the kind of work that does justify these superlatives in time. In giving we receive!

Getting Out of Hand

I never have course material sitting on the tables when participants arrive first thing on day one of a new program. I want their first experience to be connecting with the other course attendees and myself, rather than burying their noses into the course material. Of course, at some point in the morning we need to hand out the course manuals. To do this I ask the participants if they know whether the manuals have been paid for yet. This is generally met by perplexed looks. I push the point a little harder saying that I need evidence that the manuals have been paid for and if no one has brought their receipt of payment to training, then they will have to be paid for some other way. At this point I get a couple of participants up the front and hand them all the manuals. Then I instruct the remaining participants to go and 'pay' those holding the manuals a compliment in order to 'pay for' and receive one. I will also jokingly add that if the person holding the manuals doesn't rate the compliment highly enough then they should just hold on to them and encourage the person complimenting them to do better. As you can imagine this creates a lot of energy, enthusiasm and laughter. ***Compliments and praise generate warmth*** between people and are a valuable tool for connection and consequent influence.

After this exercise, I discuss with the group how the people holding the manuals felt receiving compliments - even though it was a very agenda-laden activity. There is obviously a degree of discomfort for some in the exercise but on the whole people enjoy the experience - both those giving and those receiving the compliments.

I then ask the participants to take a post-it note and write down their guess as to the magic ratio of positive to negative comments in great relationships - what amount of negativity to positivity should equate, in their thinking, to a healthy, happy and stable relationship? Dr John Gottman and his team of researchers have researched this very topic and, after observing thousands of couples over many decades, they have come up with a statistic that predicts marriage longevity and happiness according to the degree of negativity to positivity in everyday interactions. I'm surprised how often I get a few people who write down a ratio of more negative to positive comments in good marriages, however there tends to only be a few. Very few people, the minority of participants, guess that the ratio is as high as five to one. And yet this is the very least that the ratio of positivity to negativity ever is in genuinely happy marriages.

I am obviously not training my participants to have great marriages but I am training them to have great relationships in the workplace where they have influence and take influence from others. People tend to be very predictable in what does and doesn't work – across the planet and across cultures – in terms of relationships generally. And just to make us all feel better about crossing over from marriage relationship advice into business relationship advice - the Harvard Business School carried out excellent research that identified there was also a positive to negative ratio of five to one in high performing workplace teams!

It is important to let people know when they've failed to meet expectations, but if we're doing that more often than we are complimenting them and giving them positive feedback, then that habit will wear thin very quickly. ***People respond better to affirmation than they do to criticism*** even if it is constructive criticism. When we have ongoing relationship with people, there is an expectation that we will 'fill their bucket up' with praise and recognition before we 'start emptying it out' with criticism. Often people are aware of their shortcomings, but the more they get told about them, without any encouragement for their positive efforts, the less inclined they are to make the effort to change.

You'll be a better influencer of others to the extent that you are able to see what people are doing well, or simply just 'right', and show genuine appreciation for what you observe. Then when you need to influence their behavior or thinking they are in a much better frame of mind to receive what you have to say.

CHAPTER FOURTEEN

THE BIGGIES

INTRODUCTION

I called this chapter 'The Biggies' because in my three decades' experience of working in people development, I have found that these are powerful tools that we have to shift the behavior of others: Passion; Vision; Values and; Convictions. These four are truly the 'biggies' regarding influence with others because they drive us to action, and that action determines the direction of our influence on others.

I am always more interested in listening to a passionate person than a dispassionate person. Of course, passion doesn't determine whether we are correct or not - that equation needs to be resolved through other means - but passion does show us that at least the person sharing the information believes in its value. Using the analogy of a vehicle on a journey, influencing people would be the destination, and passion is the high-octane fuel in the tank that can make the vehicle go much faster and arrive at the intended destination quicker.

Vision is the ability to clearly see the end goal or the desired outcome. In relation to the analogy of the vehicle on a journey, vision allows us to see the final destination before the journey has even begun. *The clearer the vision, the greater the likelihood of influencing people toward the desired outcome,* and as with any lengthy journey, when we're aware of and have clarity regarding where we are going, then we can make decisions as to the most suitable route. As a result, we have a greater chance of anticipating, and therefore avoiding, roadblocks.

Core values and convictions are very clear road signs of where to go and where not to go on the journey of influencing others. Values and convictions are powerful signposts that communicate to us, and others, hazards, speed limits, no-go zones, and clear open highway. Before we embark on any journey, we need a reason for doing so. A journey takes time, resources, and commitment. It is important to identify a reason big enough to inspire us to make the journey towards change and see it through to the destination.

14.1

PASSION

There's just no substitute for passion. Passion is that strong feeling of enthusiasm or excitement for something that drives us towards it. It is so much easier to influence people if you have a passionate conviction – something you enthusiastically believe in. I am a naturally passionate person and I know in many ways that helps in terms of influencing others, but I've seen plenty of people with ample passion fail to shift others around them due to a lack of other relevant characteristics such as courage or conviction or emotional intelligence. But if you're going to have anything to help 'get the ball (or people) moving' then passion is one of the best places to start!

Stopping the Ball Rolling

Recently I had an opportunity to demonstrate how passionate I was about a certain issue. As someone who has played football competitively for over 45 years now, I've heard plenty of half-time talks, and a lot of irrelevant pep talks over many seasons. Impassioned encouragement at half time does play a crucial part in getting the very best out of players, but I can't tell you how many times I've heard captains say at half time that we are better than our opposition even though they are clearly dominating us on the field.

As the years roll on, it's not likely that players over the age of 40 will turn on a skilled performance in the second half if they weren't capable of it in the first half! So, given the fact of 'plateaued skills' as players age, you will never hear me criticizing a player on the field for inadequate ability because I know their skill level just can't change regardless of a berating. But one thing I do believe in is tactical strategy. At my age and stage, strategy on the field is the most significant means to influence the outcome of any game.

On this day, I was playing for a new football team and we were in the middle of a very closely fought game when the opposition scored a goal. I grabbed the ball and yelled at my team to huddle in for a team talk prior to reassembling for the kick-off. It was an unusual occurrence but I was so passionate about the goal that had just been scored due to our inadequate defense that I couldn't contain myself.

The goal that had just been scored by the opposition was from a free kick. When a free kick is given in football there are several strategical tactics that can be employed in order to reduce the opposition's advantage. If the free kick is close to the goal then it is prudent for someone on the defensive team to 'stand on the ball' (right in front of it) to make sure the opposition don't take a quick free kick and consequently gain a greater advantage through the tactic of speed. Not only did we fail to impede a quick free kick, but many of our players turned their backs to the ball to jog back into position - another elementary mistake and one that wasn't skill or fitness based.

I don't mind seeing better teams score against us, nor am I at all concerned by mistakes that lead to the ball ending up in the back of our net. Even international level players make mistakes and are outplayed by the opposition. But on this occasion, we had let in a goal by means of two very elementary errors which I knew we were capable of rectifying, so I very passionately explained to them the error of our ways and clarified the tactics we could be utilizing.

Whenever we set out to influence people, to shift them from the status quo, one of the most potent tools we can have in our arsenal is that of passion. On the football field that day I was primarily driven by passion for the fact that we were making a very elementary tactical error that could be easily corrected simply through player awareness. There were nine other players that I had to communicate with, and very little time given that we were walking back to halfway for a kick-off. I needed to communicate very strongly and assertively to the rest of my players. I had no institutional authority, but I needed to get the other players on board quickly. In this instance, it was the passion with which I called the men in and communicated to them that made them listen to a me. ***My passion gave me influence when I didn't have long term relationship or trust,*** and made all the difference to how the team proceeded towards our aim of winning the game.

14.2

VISION

Tools such as communication techniques are useful tools for influencing people, but only to the extent that you have a clear and constructive vision and purpose for the shift you're attempting to influence. Vision is vital because without knowing the destination you would like your team to journey to, you will not know which road to influence them to travel upon to get there.

Home Ground Advantage

As part of my leadership programs I will ask participants to brainstorm the attributes and characteristics of the ultimate team member. Over the years, several people have taken this simple activity back to their teams, asking their staff members what they believe are the traits of an ultimate team member, and then using the key elements to create vision statements and codes of conduct for their teams.

One leader who attended my program went home and used this activity with his family. He held a meeting with his spouse and children and asked them what would make a great family member. They all brainstormed their input and as a result each family member chose a particular characteristic that they wanted to work on to make them a 'great family member'. As a family, they made a visual display of this in their home. They now have family meetings every Wednesday at which, among other things, they discuss how each one is doing in terms of their chosen attribute. The statements that the family brainstormed now became visions for each person. They have centered their Wednesday night meetings around the revisiting of their values, so there is accountability for how they are doing with attaining their vision.

It all started with this man's vision of what he wanted his family to be, and the activity was one of the 'how's' in terms of him achieving his vision. It really has created a fantastic bond for this family and the key to the exercise happening in the first place was the leader recognizing how the exercise could be useful in helping him reach his own vision for creating a fantastic family culture. As a result, other families that are seeing their visual display have been influenced also.

This really is an impressive example of how passion and vision can cause us to recognize effective tools when we come across them that can help us to achieve our desired goals. This father already had a vision for the great family he wanted to raise so when he was exposed to the team building exercise he immediately recognized how useful it might also be outside of work. He was like a master craftsman who spotted a new, quality tool at the hardware store. The craftsman already has in mind the piece of furniture he wants to create and the material he'll make it out of, but when he spots a tool that he doesn't have like a new dovetail jig, he recognizes its potential to help him build the piece of furniture he envisages. He already has a vison for the piece and the tool is unlikely to alter that vision, but it can help him achieve his vision in a quicker and more effective way. The ability to make good use of the new tool hinges on the quality of his initial vision.

At the Earliest Date Possible

One of the factors that helped me to have a clear vision for my family and children was my work with at risk youth in my early 20's. The more I met these young people and the more I heard their stories, the more I realized that their relationships with their parents, and particularly with their fathers, was often problematic. I remember asking one group of course participants if they had ever spent quality one-on-one time with their fathers growing up. Not a single student could remember a time when their father had taken them out with the sole intention of spending quality time with them (note to dads - I'm sorry, but having your kids in the car with you while listening to the sports on the way to the hardware store, and dropping them off at the playground while you shop doesn't constitute 'quality time').

I could see what was lacking in my student's lives. I had a tangibly clear vision of what would happen if I didn't give my own children quality time, and this vision inspired me with a new vision for how I would treat my own children. Armed with this vision for raising a great family, I immediately recognized an effective tool for what I wanted to build when I spotted it in the book *The Seven Habits of Highly Effective Families* by Stephen Covey. In the book, Covey talks about dating his kids when they were younger. He suggests setting dates in an annual calendar where each child is taken out for special one-on-one time with mum or dad. Once I found this tool I booked in two dates per year with each of my children. The dates had to include some kind of outing with food like lunch or dinner and an activity of their choosing.

My children loved these times of dedicated attention and would anticipate them with great enthusiasm. When we arrived home at the end of a date, my other children would quiz them at length on where we'd been, what we had done, and most importantly, what we had eaten! I had discovered a brilliant tool that was perfect for helping me to achieve my vision of growing a close and loving family culture. To this day, even though my children are all now adults, I still occasionally 'date' them.

What happens in (Roto)Vegas

My wife and I have intentionally done a number of things with our family over the years because we have had a clear vison of what we want our children and family to look like years down the track. At the beginning of our marriage both of us were working with at-risk youth in employment programs for young people who had not done well in the school system. We also accepted a role as house parents at a home for troubled teenage girls. As young people in our early twenties with no parenting experience of our own we took on looking after teenagers whose own parents could not tolerate them due to their unruly behavior. We had no idea how difficult this would be when we took it on but we managed five years in the role before we finally left to build our own family in a more peaceful environment! The most positive personal benefit these experiences elicited was helping us to solidify as a couple a vision for how we wanted our own children to turn out, particularly when they were teenagers. This caused us to instigate a number of traditions and events designed to develop children who had great attitudes and sociably acceptable behaviors as teenagers and beyond. I'm happy to say that our efforts seemed to work!

One event we instigated was the 'RotoVegas' weekend. When our children turned ten we took them for a weekend away to another city in New Zealand called Rotorua (or more affectionately termed 'RotoVegas'). One parent and one child, one car and one set of tapes – a series developed by Dr James Dobson called 'Preparing for Adolescence'. The tapes (this was back in the era where we felt fortunate to have a 'tape deck' in our car!), covered topics such as puberty, self-esteem and peer pressure. This weekend was incredibly formative and led to many related conversations where we could talk about issues like peer pressure and pornography.

Dr James Dobson had a huge vision when he began his organization: 'Focus on the Family'. His vision was to influence and equip the families of the world to thrive. At one point, his organization had 1000 full time employees, and his daily broadcast was being heard by over 200 million people in mainland China alone. Even before I had my own children I had developed a clear vision for what I wanted my children to grow up like. People like Dr Dobson provided me with the resources to be the kind of father that I wanted to be – even though I hadn't actually experienced a father for myself. In the days before smart watches I bought myself a calculator watch and set a daily alarm on it to listen to Dr Dobson's broadcast. I had found a tool that I knew could fast track me towards my vision for my family, and I intended to make the most of it!

My wife and I shifted to Tauranga – a beautiful seaside town in New Zealand - so I could complete my business degree in my early thirties. Each day I would drop my son at day-care in the morning and then I would go and study in one of the upstairs rooms that they were gracious enough to let me use. I discovered a well-stocked library across the road with all Dr Dobson's books and I absolutely devoured every one. His books were a huge influence on me in terms of my vision for having a solid, functional family, and especially the 'how' to achieve that vision.

The tools for our journey are usually informational – but in reading his books I was also being relationally influenced by him – albeit from a far distance. The people we keep company with, and glean insight from on a regular basis, greatly influence the tools we pick up to help us reach our destinations. ***Make sure you have the best people around you,*** or influencing you (even if from afar), to help you on your journey.

No 'Arm Done

On a lighter but just as formative note, we had a rule in our household – no dating until you can beat your father in an arm wrestle! ("Your poor daughter!" I hear you say!) Obviously, this was quite a tongue in cheek rule that started out as something of a joke but it did have a much more serious concept behind its facade. Having seen the carnage that can occur with young people dating prematurely, especially with the rise of STIs (sexually transmitted infections) and unplanned preg-nancies, we were keen to steer our children towards making healthy and timely decisions in terms of dating the opposite sex. The arm wrestle rule continued as a family tradition year after year in our household. I remember finding my six-year-old daughter doing press -ups in the lounge one day and when I enquired as to what she was doing her reply was, "I'm getting stronger so I can beat you in an arm wrestle one day!"

Our family arm wrestle rule meant that we had communicated about the ideal and not so ideal circumstances around dating prior to the need of having a serious conversation about the topic. By then it can be too late when a son or a daughter has fallen madly in love with their lifelong partner at age 12. Of course, I'm joking, but teenagers can be difficult to have these kinds of conversations with once the process of infatuation has begun so it's ideal to have started them ahead of time. Our vision for helping our teenagers through those often difficult years with as little trauma as possible meant we started early developing our family culture.

If you don't have a vision for your family, for your marriage, for your financial future, for your business or your career then you are putting your hand up to becoming a victim of circumstance. As a family, we are far from perfect, but I do sincerely believe that having a long-term vision for the positive future that I wanted my children to have was a far better decision than leaving their development to the winds of change and at the mercy of life's twists and turns. And that vision paid off, as all three children have had very positive teenage years and opposite sex relationships. People who have a clear vision of the future are far more likely to see it come to pass than those who never define their vision.

Finishing on a High

I was delivering a two-day negotiation skills training course attended by some people with very strong opinions. One of the attendees was approximately six foot four in height and towered above my much shorter five foot six frame. At some point during the two-day training program he said something that I deemed worth celebrating and I put my hand up to give him a 'high-five'. My efforts at congratulating him were met with a simple stare, no movement, and a rumbling low voice stating, "I don't do high-fives."

Being someone that loves to influence others to make positive shifts I made a mental note at the time to somehow get him to give me a high-five by the conclusion of the program. You can imagine I was very disappointed when he was called away urgently early on the afternoon of the second day due to a surprise pressing commitment. I was disappointed not to have had a good attempt at achieving the goal that I had set for him.

Several months went by and I was both surprised and delighted to have the very same gentleman turn up to another training program that I was running over a slightly longer period of time. I'm not sure if he remembered the high-five incident but I certainly did the moment I saw him and made a mental commitment to reinstate the goal.

At the end of the first or second day of the new training program I was running a team initiative activity where the various participants attempted to achieve a team goal requiring them to think laterally to solve a problem. The team did really well and achieved the desired outcome with some excellent problem solving skills after just a few attempts. As a result, on the spur of the moment I asked one of the other attendees to turn towards the gentleman and give him a high-five in celebration of their achievement. The attendee that I asked to make the high-five was completely unaware of any history or context to the request and so obediently stepped forward and raised his hand in the high-five position and was met by a somewhat sluggish high-five by the gentleman, who turned and gave me a knowing smile.

We got on so well over the duration of the program that he spoke appreciatively of the change that had occurred in him both personally and professionally, and at the request of another one of the other participants at the end of the program we had our photo taken together with this giant of a man lifting me up in his arms - a dramatic transformational shift from someone with such a strong 'no high-fiving' policy. In his closing remarks to the other participants and to attending managers he spoke of how much the course had impacted his work life, his relationship with his children, and especially his relationship with his wife.

I don't achieve those kinds of results 100% of the time, but I certainly have a vision to. ***My passion drives me towards that vision, and the many influence tools I have collected over the years steer me towards a quicker fulfilment of that vision.*** Being able to challenge people towards positive change is one of those tools. I know not everyone likes the kinds of challenges that I do, but I know that inwardly we all value people taking an interest in our futures.

14.3

VALUES AND CONVICTIONS

Values and convictions are very important for me and the way that I conduct myself. I remember years ago asking a leader of young people if he had a guiding principle by which he lived, to which he answered that it would probably be the illustrious words of John Lennon; "Whatever gets you through the night is alright." To be honest, I was quite taken aback that someone in a position of influence and care in the lives of young people would opt for such a self-oriented expression as a potential guiding code to live by. What would he say to students who lied to him because they were trying to evade responsibility for a misdemeanor?

This leader had probably never really reflected on what his values were and how they were influencing his day to day decisions. It is well worth investing some time into clarifying how you want to guide your life decisions – what your value signposts will be along the road towards your life vision. The clearer your values are, and the stronger your conviction is, the more stable your foundation for influencing others towards the best possible outcome.

In training I am often asked my opinion of what people should do if the company's values differ to their own, and even more so if their manager's values contradict theirs. Certainly, the issue of the company's values being contrary to good, commonly held values is seldom an issue. It is much more likely to be the company culture that people struggle with, the 'hidden culture', such as the dishonest treatment of customers. It may be that their manager's personal values clash with their own and they end up raising the issue on training with me. In most cases the values clash is not a 'game changer' and it is up to the team member to influence their manager's behavior to better line up with the organization's values. In a much smaller number of cases the values clash is so jarring that once the staff member has attempted to shift their boss to no avail, then they may be left with no option but to hand in their notice and seek employment where there is a better fit in terms of their values.

Holding a Gun to their Head

In the book *Unbroken*, the biography of Olympic runner and Japanese prisoner of war detainee Louis Zamperini, the story is told of Louie and his comrades being attacked by an air bombardment, on a small island atoll, as a reprisal for their attack on a similar Japanese base. For some reason the men were unprepared for this stinging counter-attack and completely taken by surprise in the early hours of the morning. The base was not designed to withstand a significant assault from the air so there were no purpose-built air raid shelters or even obvious places for people to take refuge during the onslaught. Men took shelter around the base of coconut trees, dug their own shelters with their bare hands, and one man even ran off the end of the island taking shelter in the water. Several men took shelter under a military lorry until it disintegrated when a bomb hit it.

The island had a small indigenous population who took shelter in their most significant building - a sturdily built church. One of Louie's compatriots, knowing that this would be an obvious target for the Japanese, ran into the church and yelled at the people to evacuate it. When he was unsuccessful in his attempts to shift them, he pulled out his side arm and threatened to shoot them if they didn't leave the premises. They were much quicker to oblige under the threat of being executed and it was to the credit of this man that he thought so quickly on his feet because the church was absolutely obliterated during the air attack, and he was therefore directly responsible for saving the lives of all the people that he had forced out of the church.

This story is a vivid illustration of the fact that there are times when our influence of others seems unduly coercive or even abusive from the perspective of the ones being influenced. It serves as a fantastic example of someone being so certain of what is best for the group in the circumstance that he was even prepared to appear as if he was willing to take their lives to make them do what was in their best interests. He valued the lives of these people and he was prepared to do whatever it took to maintain that value.

I am always more willing to listen to, and be influenced by, someone who has strong convictions and personal values that resonate with mine. In fact, more than just a resonance, I admire and respect people whose behavior is values-driven. That's not to say that I'm able to be influenced by anyone with any conviction, because of course it is possible to be passionately sincere and at the same time sincerely misled or delusional. Conviction of belief, and having clear ethics and principles, are very useful signposts along our journey towards influencing others.

Adding Fuel to the Fire

One of my convictions is that people should be valued and cared for, and the care of others involves making sure their work environments are healthy and safe. I pulled into a gas station very early one morning to fill up on the way to work. As I walked across the forecourt to go and pay for my gas I spotted, for the first time in my life, a customer smoking next to his vehicle. He was obviously with a crew of other guys and as I walked past him I said, "Mate - I really strongly want to suggest that you don't smoke on the forecourt because it's dangerous for yourself and everyone else!" He stared at me blankly as if I had spoken in a foreign language to him. My suggestion had absolutely zero impact. I walked into the gas station and noticed one of his crew-members and said to him, "Hey, it would be a really good idea if you could suggest to your friend that he doesn't smoke on the forecourt", to which his colleague replied, "We've tried numerous times before to tell him not to smoke at gas stations but he refuses to listen to us!"

Quite frankly I just wanted to pay for my gas and get out of there as quickly as I could, not wanting to end up on the evening news as their headline story. The customer service person behind the counter was more interested in selling me chocolate than in the potential for his workplace exploding. I try to avoid eating sugar in my diet so I countered what I thought were his sales efforts. In the end however he informed me that I had won a spot prize of two chocolate bars and he insisted I take them. I finally capitulated and took the two bars as I raced out the doors to escape the hazardous petrol station. I immediately bumped into the crewmember I had earlier been talking to. I quickly grasped an opportunity to accelerate positive change and, thrusting the chocolate bars into his hands I said, "Go and give these to your mate and ask him to please to stop smoking on the forecourt!"

As I was getting back in my car the 'smoker' walked up to me holding the two chocolate bars and asked, "Are these from you?" "Yes, they are", I replied. "Why did you give them to my mate to give to me?" he asked, clearly having put out his cigarette. "Because I just really want you to go home safely to your family at the end of this day. I want that for all of us, to go home in one piece and if you're prepared to put out your cigarette then I'm prepared to give you chocolate!" He smiled ever so slightly as we parted ways.

Sometimes our need to influence others is solely motivated for their own safety and the safety of others. It doesn't necessarily make the task of influencing the person any easier, but it does provide ample motivation on the part of the influencer. What better reason to step out on a limb and risk rejection than the motivation that we might maintain the well-being of another member of the human race, even to the extent of preserving their life. It was not only important for my safety and for the safety of the man who was smoking on the forecourt of the petrol station, but it was also important for the safety of everyone else both inside and outside the premises.

One of the things that I said to the smoker at the conclusion of our brief encounter was that I really wanted him to go home safely to his family at the end of the day. When it comes to safety it's worthwhile thinking about the bigger picture, because often that can be the tipping point in the influence of others. In my small way, I was helping him to consider the fact that his irresponsible behavior was not only putting other people at jeopardy including his fellow crew members and other patrons at the gas station, but in the unfortunate event of an explosion his behavior would have had an impact on those people who knew and loved them all – which when you think about it, would amount to hundreds of people.

My first efforts to curb the smoker's behavior were met with resistance - bordering on contempt. If one tool fails to work to influence someone, try another! If direct communication doesn't work, encouragement and generosity might. I took the opportunity with the chocolate, primarily because I was still concerned at his blasé attitude, and I was still motivated to shift his thinking. ***When safety is of primary concern, it pays to persevere,*** and when safety is an issue in the workplace it is imperative that you persevere.

Like a Red Flag to a Bull

Some time ago the (then) Prime Minister of New Zealand, the Right Honorable John Key, proposed a change to our national flag. He was personally keen to see a shift away from the current flag of the day to something that included the 'Silver Fern'- the underside of the frond of one of our native plants and the symbol used by many of our representative sports teams including the All Blacks, our champion rugby team. Choices for various alternatives were produced, and one was chosen by public referendum to go head-to-head with our current flag. In the end the nation voted to maintain the status quo and keep our existing flag.

Several months later I was in Australia at a conference and a conference delegate struck up a conversation with me about the failed attempt to change our national flag. He was disappointed that as a nation we had not been able to see the wisdom of moving to a new flag design that, in his opinion, more accurately represented our nation as opposed to our current flag which is dominated by the union Jack, the flag of England. He was particularly disappointed because of his enthusiasm to see Australia's flag change and he thought the process might be easier if New Zealand had already progressed positively down the same track.

The conference I was at was attended by people who are, generally speaking, very progressive thinkers, open to change, and probably not hugely conservative in nature. In fact, many of the attendees were known as 'Thought Leaders' internationally. It was a conference of go-getters and trendsetters. The gentleman was therefore quite surprised and possibly even shocked to hear that I had voted to keep the flag without change. You know those awkward moments in conversations when one of the parties has assumed that the other agrees, only to find out that quite the opposite is the case. He informed me that he was astonished at my stance given that in his opinion, "New Zealand had been unwilling to grow up" by refusing to adopt the new flag.

To his credit, he was interested in how I could conclude that it was better to maintain the status quo rather than shifting to something new. I did have robust thinking on the matter which I then began to share with him. Interestingly, I didn't set out to change his mind, or even influence his thinking, I merely expressed my honest stance on the issue which was unique to my own personal circumstances. I explained that I had been attending ANZAC (Australia and New Zealand Army Corps) Day parades for the last 15 years. I asked him if Australia was the same as New Zealand where dawn ANZAC parades have been progressively increasing in public attendance over the last two decades (an interesting phenomenon given that so many of those attending don't have any personal experience of the World Wars). I then went on to say that my own personal experience was one of growing up in a family with very little in the way of traditions or connection to generations past. For me personally having a family myself and creating traditions and legacy has meant an increasing desire to anchor my current reality into my national history. I was looking for historic anchors to my very transient existence, and so our national flag which was fought under, and under which so many people died, has become more and more meaningful to me as I've aged.

This attendee could relate strongly to the sense of connection that I felt with those who had fought and died on behalf of both our nations. They concluded the conversation with me by stating that they still felt a lean towards replacing the current Australian flag but they were now much more sympathetic to the other side of the debate having heard my reasons for not wanting change.

Passion, vision, values and convictions. When we align these four mechanisms in our own lives, we streamline our journey towards easier and more effective influence in other's lives. Passion is a driving force that helps people to understand why it is important that they should take influence from us. Vision is the rationale and guide for that influence - it allows us to see where taking of influence will get us. Values keep us on track to reaching that vision and protect us from taking the wrong kind of influence, and convictions align us with the right kind of influence.

CHAPTER FIFTEEN

TRUST

"Trust is the core currency of all human relationships."
Glen Sharkey

INTRODUCTION

Trust is a primary element in successful human relationships. If influence is a natural component in all relationships, both in the workplace and the non-work environment, then trust is naturally the core factor when attempting to influence people for the greater good.

In her new book *Presence*, Amy Cuddy says people quickly answer two questions in their heads when they first meet you: "Can I respect this person?" and "Can I trust this person?" Cuddy says that you won't get far in your efforts to influence someone if they don't trust you. In fact, efforts to influence without trust might come across as manipulative and create suspicion. Warm, strong people may elicit admiration but it is only when trust is established through experience and time that you will shift from being a threat to being an influencer.

RELATIONAL ACCOUNTING

In my leadership training I call this concept of creating trust 'Relational Accounting' - the metaphorical accounts that we have with people that are either in surplus or in deficit. Deposits will decrease the deficit and increase the surplus and in the same way withdrawals will deplete a surplus or increase an account already in deficit.

Many behaviors amount to relational deposits, including: ***acts of kindness, giving assistance, recognizing endeavor, keeping promises, and sincere apologies***. In the same way, relational withdrawals can include: ***pettiness and harshness, withholding assistance, undue criticism, failing to keep promises, being arrogant and conceited, defensiveness and arrogantly blaming others***. Deposits are the 'Above the Line' behaviors, and withdrawals are the 'Below the Line' behaviors.

The one common factor of all these deposits and withdrawals is that they all accomplish the building or diminishing of trust. Trust is the key relational currency and the more I am considered to be trustworthy by someone, the greater my capacity to have influence with that person. Conversely, the more I trust someone the more open I am to their influence.

The (Micro)Scope of the Job

A woman on one of my leadership courses approached me during a lunchtime break stating that she had had enough of her manager and was ready to quit. She informed me that her manager was micromanaging her and she was finding it intolerable. What would you say to someone like that?

She was obviously upset, visibly frustrated and ready to phone her manager and quit her job on the spot. The first question I asked her was, "Do you really want to leave the job?" She replied that she did, but that it was only because she was finding the situation untenable. If the situation improved she would not want to leave. That initial question for me was helpful in establishing her level of motivation and commitment to any solutions we might discuss. I had limited time in which to make suggestions for her and if she had no intrinsic desire to retain the job, irrespective of micromanagement, then it wasn't good use of my time to formulate a possible solution with her.

On the leadership course, we had already covered the need to take ownership and responsibility for issues that were not going well, so I discussed with her the approach that I suggest in many of these kinds of situations where direct reports are raising issues with their up-line management that may solicit a less-than-positive response.

I began by asking her how she thought the manager might respond to the suggestion that he was micromanaging her. She thought that he would quite likely get defensive, and when I asked her why, she thoughtfully considered the question and then responded that the term 'micromanagement' was a derogatory comment on his leadership. She realized that her language could potentially make her communication come across as contemptuous. So, we discussed alternative language that was less inflammatory. The biggest question I wanted her to consider was what she thought was causing her manager to micromanage her. She concluded that it was a lack of trust. I suggested to her

that *the more she could take responsibility and ownership for the issue of lack of trust, the more likely she was to get a positive outcome*.

This woman then went to see her manager and talked the problem through with him. She was careful to omit the word
'micromanagement' from the conversation, and she set her tone to be
neutral and non-judgmental. She suggested to her manager that because he was spending so much time watching over her work that she
wondered if he had an issue of trust in her ability. He responded somewhat defensively to this suggestion, but she continued the conversation
without an accusatory tone and instead said to him that she wondered
if it wasn't so much his issue, but rather her issue for being inade-
quately trustworthy in some areas. She took full ownership for the issue of untrustworthiness and asked him in what areas he needed her to
become more trustworthy.

This tactic changed the manager's response to her entirely, and
instead of having to defend himself, he began to think through the
ways in which she could improve her trustworthiness with him which
meant she was able to leave the conversation knowing which facets
she could work on. In the process, he also was prompted to think about
his own reactions to feeling unsure of her abilities and it clarified a
way forward to building greater trust in the work relationship. Once
she had followed through on his suggestions and became more trustworthy she naturally received less 'micro-management' from him.

The outcome of this conversation was a win/win. She had
something that she wanted to get out of the conversation, namely to
move towards less micromanagement from her manager, but she was
also able to consider the issue from his point of view. For her to be

able to increase her own trustworthiness with her manager would benefit him by saving him time and effort watching over her work. The conversation went much better than she had anticipated. ***By planning the conversation ahead of time, she was able to influence the outcome*** both by thinking through the situation from his point of view and working out what she was willing to take ownership for that she could change herself in the situation. As a result, she continued on very happily in her job.

15.2

EARNING TRUST

Is trust is given or earned? In my opinion it is both. When someone starts in a new work role they are automatically given a degree of trust. As human beings, we can't operate without a base level of trust. We learn this trust through repeated life experiences from birth onwards. We learn to trust that our needs will be met, that we can stand on two feet, that our voice will be heard, and so on, until with repeated successes over the years we no longer need to re-establish basic trust with every new encounter. As a trainer, I trust that my students will turn up on day one, and I trust that in an emergency they will behave appropriately. I also trust that though they might make mistakes, they have not generally done so with malicious intent. Therefore, I give them a degree of trust from the start.

To borrow from an analogy I first developed years ago when coaching challenging pre-teens, it is as if a person begins a new work role with a glass jar a quarter filled with marbles. The amount of marbles in the jar represents the amount of trust the employee has in the 'relational bank account' with their employer. This trust is there simply on the basis of common human trust in others. From then on, the 'Trust Jar' has marbles added to it through positive behaviors and interactions, or marbles are taken from it based on negative behaviors and interactions of the new team member.

Trust diminishes or increases dependent on the negative withdrawals or positive additions of the team member. It increases when we exhibit 'Above the Line' behaviors, and it decreases when we show 'Below the Line' behaviors.

A key component of leading is delegating tasks. Trust is at the heart of the vast majority of decisions related to delegation. If it appears that a team member isn't trustworthy to perform a delegated task then it is their responsibility to become more trustworthy in their leader's eyes. The leader can't do that for them. What a leader can do though is to explain to the team member in what ways they aren't as trustworthy as they need to be (the current marble total), what the required level of trustworthiness needs to be (the target marble total), and especially what's required to get there (how to add more marbles).

The previous story about the young, micromanaged employee is an example of someone influencing up – influencing her manager – by taking responsibility for what she could change. She could have become embittered by what she couldn't change – or by what she felt her manager should change – but by being empowered to change what she could, and communicating this clearly and without judgement to her manager, she was able to get a win/win in the situation.

It should not be lost on us that her manager also had to take responsibility or his own need to change as well because he had failed to paint a clear picture to his employee of what he needed from her - what that looked like in relation to her current work levels, and what she needed to do to improve. That was his responsibility in terms of influencing her. Trust is always a two-way street. It only occurs when both parties are willing for it to occur. Good will must go both ways.

I work with a number of leadership models in my training such as motivation, communication, delegation, and teambuilding. Invariably the issue of trust is intrinsic to every one of these models, because trust is the key currency of relationships. ***When trust is improved working relationships improve.*** And of course, the converse is true - when trust is diminished working relationships become more difficult and problematic, and the ability to influence loses necessary traction.

When I am trusted, I feel motivated, but when those around me lack trustworthiness, my trust in them naturally diminishes and with it my motivation. The more I trust someone, the better the quality of our communication, and conversely the less I trust someone or am not trusted by them, the poorer the quality of our communication. Teams that have high levels of trust are more productive, solve problems quicker, and generally get things done faster than teams who have significant trust issues. And as discussed earlier, my ability to delegate work tasks to others essentially comes down to the issue of trust.

Building trust with others is vital to enduring success in every area of our lives. Caring for people isn't just a personal value I hold, it has now become a value that businesses need to also invest into as social media creates increasing transparency in the workplace. If a business is not genuine in its care for its customers, it is becoming more and more difficult to hide this from the wider public. And if a customer doesn't feel that the business is serving their needs they will lose trust in the business, and be less inclined to patronize the business.

CHAPTER SIXTEEN

THE POWER OF CARING

"People don't care how much you know,
until they know how much you care."
Theodore Roosevelt

INTRODUCTION

There can be **no greater motivator to influence others than caring about them**. In my training, I am often charged by the management of companies to influence their staff in terms of behavior and attitude. I know that there are some facilitators who observe my day-one practice of really getting to know the participants, and who think this takes far too long and cuts into valuable course content time. However, I find this time indispensable as a foundation for earning the right, in subsequent training days, to question people's behavior and attitudes and suggest alternatives for change. Without investing into the genuine care of the people I am working with, I can't expect to have a great deal of influence with them.

UNDER LOCK AND THE KEY TO SUCCESS

A question I am sometimes asked is whether there are some participants in my training who I am genuinely unable to influence in any way at all. The honest answer is that occasionally I feel like I achieve very little transformational change with possibly one or two participants per year. I consider it part of my job in leading and influencing my training participants to have the belief that everyone can change, you just have to know how to unlock them – how to open the door of influence in their life.

To use the analogy of 'unlocking people', I could approach a door with five keys in my hand aiming to try all of them if necessary to unlock the door. Not everyone has 'locks on the doors' of their lives. Some people are very open to change, very open to new information, and are excited about being challenged to grow and develop. Other people have a few locks on their doors, some of which are always locked, and others which may only lock in certain threatening circumstances. And lastly there are some people who have numerous locks on their door that have been rusted shut and that require numerous keys and numerous unlocking attempts to open them up.

Often the day one activities that I get people to participate in on my training are enough to unlock most of my attendees but there are always a few diehards that take longer to thaw out than the others. With them I'm particularly looking for *the right keys to utilize to open them up*, and care is indispensable in this process.

Holding them Hostage

Years ago, I had a 'hostage' on a leadership training program. He was resistant to being on the course and to the homework that was required to be completed to achieve the National Qualification that the course was delivering. He was so resistant that when his manager refused to allow him to miss a day of training because of work pressure, he ignored his manager and failed to attend that day.

One morning a few weeks later he made it back to my training class and I heard him talking to some other participants about the troubles that he was going through with his teenage son, so I gently enquired about this at morning tea. We discussed how traumatic it had been for him with late-night calls from the police due to his son's troubled behavior, even to the point where the father had been beaten by the son on more than one occasion. Having worked with at-risk youth in the past I was able to empathize with him in the first instance, but also give him meaningful support and advice. My conversation was founded in genuine care for his traumatic situation, and I could tell he really appreciated my heartfelt interest.

The course required us to be together for one day per month and each time thereafter I would quiz him first thing in the morning as to how things were going with his son and his family who were all being impacted by the son's dysfunctional behavior. Because this was the most major 'pain point' in his life, and as a result of the simple interest that I took in his personal circumstance, his attitude towards the program took a 180° turn to the point where he looked forward attending the course. By the time the course finished he was also the first to complete all of his required assessment homework prior to the last day. It certainly wasn't my aim to show an interest in his story in an effort to unlock him to the course content. It is, however, a natural outcome of caring for people that they become increasingly open to your influence and it certainly makes the road of shifting people an easier one when it's built on the foundation of care.

Flying off the Handle

I was at a regional airport that was under refurbishment and as a result their baggage collection area had been temporarily shifted outside the front of the terminal. This meant that it encroached into the parking area and a thoroughfare road. A woman had parked her car beside the temporary fencing of the baggage collection area, and as a result she had inadvertently caused a road block holding up other vehicles trying to get out of the rental car area. The baggage overseer came striding over to her and in a menacingly irritated voice yelled, "Hey lady - you can't park there – get your car out of the way!!" *There was no sense of care in his tone or in his attitude whatsoever.* There was no indication that he was concerned for her vehicle or for the egress of other roadway users. The only obvious sense was that he was annoyed and frustrated (possibly by the

IT IS A NATURAL OUTCOME OF CARING FOR PEOPLE THAT THEY BECOME MORE OPEN TO YOUR INFLUENCE.

angst that the temporary system was causing) and that it was 'all about him'. In this case, the baggage overseer was able to get the woman to shift her vehicle, but only because of his positional authority rather than any relational authority that he had earnt with her.

When we influence people without any sense of care on our part, or more importantly, leave them with no sense that we care about them, we often achieve a ***short-term gain at the expense of a long-term pain***. This handler got a driver to shift her car in the short term, but he had exposed his anger issues to everyone watching on and that could come back to haunt him in the future. It would have been just as easy, and better for the brand of the airport, for him to have shown some care for the customer and achieved the same result but without risking damage to his own, or the airport's, reputation.

Caring for people is such a foundational issue when it comes to influencing others. I know personally I am much more likely to be influenced by other people when they show some care and interest in me as a person and my needs, than I am to be influenced by people who are only interested in achieving their own agenda, regardless of the impact on our short or long term relationship.

Giving Up Without a Fight

I had been playing football for a short time with a new team so I was conscious that I was a new comer to their team culture and needed to understand and, to some extent, comply with that culture. During one game two members of the opposition football team became upset with each other. One had expected the other to pass the ball to him and when it didn't happen the former abused and eventually kicked his fellow team member. The cultural norm on the football field in New Zealand is to let them fight it out and hopefully one or both of the fighting team will be sent off the field, giving the non-violent team a decided advantage. At the very least it would be the norm to let them argue because that means their unity as a team has been unsettled, which will prove a disadvantage for them when they returned to the game. While I wasn't sure exactly what my new team's culture was in regard to this kind of behavior, I was aware that it's ***not my culture*** to let fighting exist when I can do something about it. So, I quickly moved in between these two angry opposition team members, holding them apart, and suggesting that they settle down for their own sake and for the sake of their team. My intervention was all it took to lower their blood pressure (and their testosterone) and get them back to doing what we had come to do.

In a small way, I know I was influencing the culture of my team with my own personal values and ethos. I wasn't surprised at the instant influence I was able to have with the opposition team members, because ultimately, I was simply giving them a chance to slow down and make a rational choice that the heat of the moment had deprived them of. Most people, ***when they stop to analyze their behavior, would rather be interacting in a positive way than in a negative way,*** and most people have a deep internal need for others to care about the painful experiences in life that they are facing.

16.2

CARE – THE FINAL WORD

My 'Care Model' is one that I consistently highlight at the end of all my leadership training programs. Many of those courses conclude with leaders from the workplace delivering presentations on projects that they have been working on during the course. The projects are often company-wide improvement projects so by the time we have listened to the project presentations by each of the participants, speeches by management, and a simple graduation including the presentation of certificates, I am very wary of taking up too much more time. As a result, I have developed a very succinct closing message which centers around four concentric circles, all of which I draw on the whiteboard as I speak.

I begin by saying that although we have covered a lot of ground during the training covering numerous areas of content, I want to attempt to **sum up the program with one small word: 'Care'**. I then draw the first large circle and label it the 'The Customer'. I inform those present that we must never cease to stop caring for the customer or the client because they are the reason for our business's existence. Then inside that circle I drew another circle and label it 'The Company'. I speak briefly about the need for us to maintain our 'Care Factor' in terms of the organization that we work for, and if our care drops for the business then we need to do what's necessary to get it back up to an acceptable level. It is detrimental to the business and to our own satisfaction in our work if we lose care for the business's success and worse still, become antagonistic towards its success.

The next concentric circle I draw inside 'The Company' circle is 'The Team' circle. I tell the participants that their job as leaders in the business is to always care about their team. All elements of effective leadership stem from this core motive. When your team thrives, the company thrives and the customer benefits as a result.

With minimal room left at the center of those three circles I ask the audience, "Who is at the center of all these circles?" To which people usually reply, "We are!" More important than the customer, the company, or their team, is the need to care about themselves and look after their well-being physically in terms of diet and exercise, emotionally, intellectually, and spiritually (to the extent that they recognize spirituality as a valid part of their lives). If we aren't functioning well, we can't lead well. However, I say that *they are not actually number one*, and that there is someone or some people who are actually more important than we are. Normally at this point one or more people will call out; "My spouse or partner", or, "Our families." I will entirely agree with them and say that that's exactly right, we are not number one, our loved ones are, whoever they may be. When we put ourselves first at the expense of putting our loved ones second, we end up losing out ourselves in the process. When we prioritize our close relationships and the care we give them, we always end up improving our own life.

The Dunedin study, (along with numerous other studies), showed this to be the case. Children who grew up in families where their care was prioritized by their care givers, tended to also give this same care to their own families. Even though they were prioritizing their loved ones, they had a much easier run at being successful, happy, healthy and influential in the bigger scheme of things. Care for others meant they felt cared for themselves, and feeling cared for is a huge factor in our overall success and achievement in life.

I then write up my vehicle's license plate next to the concentric circles which reads 'SHRKY2'. I tell them that there is a reason why I don't have the 'SHRKY1' license plate - because my wife does. I gave her the license plate as a gift so that it could be tangible reminder to me that as important as I am, and as important as the need to care about and look after myself is, the need to look after those who are closest to me is more important. ***When we maintain a high 'Care Factor' for our loved ones, we are more likely to feel good about ourselves*** and in turn we are more likely to have a higher care factor for our team, the business or organization that we part of, and ultimately the end consumers of our products or services.

At the heart of being able to positively influence others, is the need to care about people. I consider the ability to influence others devoid of a sense of care to be poor practice at best and destructive, unethical or illegal at worst. I would hope therefore that as you read the stories, anecdotes, and principles regarding influencing others you would always consider them in the light of the bigger picture of caring for those around us.

16.3

THE PRIVILEGE OF INFLUENCE

It is a powerful and weighty responsibility to wield influence upon another person. No wonder humans create expectations and antecedents around who they will allow that privilege. The people who influence us take credit out of, or put credit into, our relational bank accounts. We are wise to guard our relational bank accounts just as we guard every valuable investment in our lives. ***The giving and taking of influence are the basis of relationships***, and relationships are as basic to our humanity as breathing and eating. So, the ability to influence well is a vital skill, not only in our career paths, but in the whole of our lives.

ABOUT THE AUTHOR

Glen Sharkey is a professional keynote speaker and training facilitator with over thirty years' experience in the people development industry. His passion is empowering people and transforming culture and he is sort after for his ability to connect quickly with his audience. He uses humor and sharp insight to take people on a journey to change and betterment and the results of his work create noticeable changes in business's efficiency and productivity. Glen was awarded "New Zealand Educator of the Year 2015/2016" in honor of his achievements.

Glen lives in New Zealand where he speaks across the nation as well as travelling abroad for speaking and training engagements. He is currently the NSANZ President and is vested in helping others' businesses to thrive. If you would like to book Glen for a speaking engagement or to facilitate training within your business you can connect with him via his website: **www.glensharkey.com**